TURNING POINTS

JULIA OGILVY

LION

To the loves of my life:
James, Flora and Alexander

In memory of
Cameron and Hayden Lord

CONTENTS

Acknowledgments

This book is about people and their stories. Some I know well and others simply intrigued me. They became part of my own journey as I explored the impact of turning points in people's lives. I am immensely grateful to all those who allowed me into their world and shared many of their innermost thoughts and emotions.

This book would not have happened without my stay on Skye in 2006 and the encouragement I got from Stevie Siegerson, Willie McIntosh and the wonderful team at Columba 1400, as well as the joy of being with the young people from Wester Hailes. The long car journey home with Colette Douglas Home and Kate Mavor and the enthusiasm of my darling husband gave me all the impetus I needed to get to work. My deepest thanks to Gay and Charlie and all of the Lord family (who are our family too) for their encouragement and support and willingness to relive the sadness at the heart of this book.

Friends like Jerry de Groot, Sharon Roe, Bruce Rigdon, Susan Golden and Mark Douglas Home have been wonderful advisers along the way. Hannah Hurley was an excellent researcher and Marjorie Bruce a brilliant transcriber. I owe so many thanks to my agents Maggie Pearlstine and Jamie Crawford for their enthusiasm, to Matt Bayliss and Brian Hunt, to Ian McAteer and Jenny Kelloe at The Union, to Sarah Warren and Stephanie Heald and to Kate, Julie, Miranda, Rhoda and the staff at Lion Hudson.

I have many happy memories of my business career before my own turning point and owe many thanks to Naim, Richard, Vicky, Jonathan, Nell, Stephen, Malcolm, Denzil, Jamie, Jill, Pippa, Charlotte, my 'landlady' Kate and so many others for all the support, belief and laughter. In recent years I have been lucky enough to have mentors and friends like Stuart Mitchell, Norman Drummond, Tom Farmer, John Moorhouse, Ian Chisholm and Stuart Miller, to whom I owe so much. My life-changing trips to Medjugorje have been the gift of Kristina Rogge, Charlotte de Klee, Matthew Proctor, Father Michael and the Sivric family as well as my dearest friends Fi and Tamara, and I am lucky enough to have the fellowship now of Holy Trinity Church in St Andrews. I am also eternally grateful to those who helped develop ProjectScotland, particularly Jack, Neville, Graeme, Euan, Colette, Ian, Kate, Susan and Rucelle, and all those who work tirelessly every day for our volunteers. My thanks too to Sharon, Alison and Pete for their loyalty to our family and to the many families and friends who keep our life full of joy. I am always inspired by the love and friendship of my prayer group – Sarah, Tamara, Charlotte, Fiona and Bridie – and all the other remarkable women in my life.

But above all, my thanks to my family: my loving husband and children, my sisters Eleanor and Charlotte and their families, my grandparents, my much loved in-laws and my parents Jill and Charles, who have all taught me so much and been there when they were needed.

PROLOGUE

Cameron Lord was an angel. How else would you explain the impact of her brief and magical appearance on this earth?

Born in Boston, Massachusetts on 4 May 1999 to Charlie and Blyth Lord, Cameron was a beautiful blonde baby, a sister for their daughter Taylor. Charlie recalls thinking at her birth that her life would be extraordinary, and indeed her first weeks of life were full of joy for everyone. But that happiness was shattered only five months later when the family learned that Hayden, her eighteen-month-old cousin, had been diagnosed with Tay-Sachs disease.

Hayden had not been well for a while, but doctors were slow to diagnose a disease most commonly found in those of Jewish extraction, which did not apply in this case. Tay-Sachs is an incurable genetic illness that causes children to die slowly and painfully by the age of four or five, never learning to walk or talk. They become blind, deaf and are unable to swallow. Terrifying seizures and bouts of pneumonia punctuate their short lives. Hayden's devoted grandparents wrote: 'This is the beginning of a long struggle that we will have to help his parents endure.'

The particular significance of this diagnosis for Cameron's parents was that her father and Hayden's father were identical twin brothers and carried the same gene. The odds that both brothers would have married wives with this rare gene were slight; that both would then go on to have an affected child were beyond measure. Tragically, they would not beat those odds.

Blyth felt devastated by the news of Hayden's diagnosis and was scared for his parents, Tim and Aliey, yet began to worry that she herself could be a carrier and that her precious daughter Cameron might have the same condition. Cameron began to show a marked startle reflex, a possible symptom, and then blood tests revealed the news they dreaded. Blyth recalls literally 'writhing on the floor at home, finding it physically unbearable that the child she was still nursing was going to die', not knowing how to tell Charlie's parents that they were to lose a second grandchild. From then on, all priorities, all of life, would change.

In August 2000, Cameron had a special holiday on the American island of Nantucket with all generations of her family around her. Her beauty was startling, breathtaking, and yet her senses were starting to shut down. She was suffering increasingly from fits and was no longer able to communicate properly. She was invited to a christening party and lay in her beautiful pale blue floral dress in a chair at one end of the room being fed from her special bottle. Barely able to swallow her liquid food, she kept those around her calm by never crying or struggling. Her gentleness and serenity gave an impression of an extraordinary inner life and wisdom beyond her years.

Her father Charlie remembers her last, tender gesture before the full throes of her first seizure would take away her ability to communicate physically: 'She reached up and stroked my cheek as if to say all would be well. It is hard to explain but somehow you knew that she was at peace, that her death was not something to fear. As it got close to the end of her life, friends recall our home being awash with a special aura; her spirit seemed to bring peace to the whole house.' Cameron died peacefully at home on 9 May 2001, four months after her cousin Hayden.

The Ogilvy family has been a part of the Lord family for over twenty years now since we met in St Andrews, and we have always shared summers together on Nantucket Island. I was the one who fed her that special day and it changed my life forever. It was a turning point that started me on an extraordinary journey of discovery. Somehow that simple moment with Cameron challenged me to think about my life and my future, to take the opportunity to make more of the life that I had been given. She is my guardian angel, appearing in my dreams, laughing and smiling and acting as a kind of 'moral compass' for all who knew her.

1

MY STORY

I remember every detail of the moment when I heard that two-year-old Cameron Lord had died. I can still feel the physical pain, the sobs that left me gasping for breath. She wasn't my child, but in her short life I had come to love her as if she was. She was my turning point, leading me to leave a successful business career and to live life differently.

I was born into a happy middle-class English family. My father was a successful businessman who commuted to the City from our pretty thatched-roof house in an Essex village, and my mother devoted herself to bringing up her three daughters. We roamed around the countryside on bicycles, learned respect for institutions such as the monarchy and values like honesty, fairness, loyalty, hard work and a sense of duty to others. Life revolved around the church, and Christmas would often be shared with elderly neighbours who lived alone.

I was eventually sent to board at a Norfolk prep school and then to the leading girls' school Wycombe Abbey, where I struggled to achieve credibility and confidence and find true friendship as most teenagers do, but there was nothing out of the ordinary about these years. There followed an exceptionally happy time at St Andrews University, and within a few days of arriving there I had met the man who was to become my husband, my guide and support through all the challenging times in my life. James was known among students for his association with the Royal Family and so his interest took me by surprise. In July 1988, we married in a local church close to my childhood home at a magical service attended by the Queen and the Princess of Wales. The town was turned upside down by police, photographers and onlookers, giving us a brief moment of celebrity, which we were glad to leave behind.

I had an exciting job as PR Manager at Garrard, the Crown Jewellers in London, and life seemed almost too good to be true. We enjoyed the parties and glamour that came with my job but soon yearned to leave the stress of urban life behind. Eventually James accepted a job in Edinburgh, and in 1991 we moved to a house near the sea in Fife. I commuted to London until I was offered the job of Managing Director of the near-bankrupt Edinburgh jewellers Hamilton and Inches. At twenty-seven, I felt ridiculously young for this responsibility and worried that I ought to be starting a family, but my charming and forceful boss Naim Attallah had seen potential and believed I was the one to turn the business around.

So began some of the happiest years of my working life. I relished every minute of the challenge, using my marketing skills to upgrade and rebrand a famous name in Scotland. I adored some of the eccentric characters in the jewellery trade and was surrounded by an impressive and loyal team. I worked all hours and became more and more wrapped up in my career. In 1994 our daughter Flora was born, and at first I managed to balance her needs with my job. I had struggled with feeling unwell throughout the pregnancy but found it hard to relinquish any business control even when I was meant to be on maternity leave. But for a while everything seemed manageable.

All this began to change in 1996. A number of factors started to complicate life. Hamilton and Inches was owned by the Asprey Group, and for some years I had enjoyed a fun and easy relationship with my boss Naim in London, who admired our business success and gave us plenty of independence. This changed when the Group was sold in 1995 and Naim left. I was needed in London more and more often and soon realized that things were going to be very different.

During this time, I was pregnant with my second child, Alexander. James had started a publishing business, which took up most of his time. Flora was adorable but waking early, and I could feel my well-planned life starting to collapse around me. Alexander, like Flora before him, was born by emergency Caesarean, and I wondered if I was really going to cope.

The tension between my loyalty to my business and the need to care for my family was severely tested when Alexander was ten weeks old. I was battling hard to retain Hamilton and Inches' independence and made a decision to rush to London to fight our corner at a budget meeting. This meant the family coming too. I remember leaving my son at my parents' house looking distinctly unwell, and by the end of the day James and I were tearing across London to the station, trying to make it in time to join Alexander in an ambulance carrying him to intensive care. As he succumbed to bronchiolitis, I sat with him through the night and for the first time felt a physical agony deep inside that this beautiful baby boy might die. I agonized for my parents who had had to deal with this trauma, and realized that my priorities had got seriously muddled. Thankfully, our son soon recovered. I didn't make any change at this point as I was soon overtaken with new concerns about the business.

By 1998 I was leading a management buyout, determined to take most of the responsibility on my shoulders in order to leave my colleagues running the company effectively. I was lucky to have our wonderful nanny, Sharon, and a loyal husband who would put up with late-night discussions during the secretive negotiations. It felt good to be able to stand up to the ranks of City lawyers that were sent our way, and I was proud of the deal we made. I simply hadn't thought of the consequences of owning the business and the feeling of being trapped that I would soon experience.

The next year was one of the hardest for me. The deal had been done, but during that time I had lost my beloved grandfather and had had no time to mourn. I missed his gentle concern that I was working too hard and not enjoying life, and his pride in his great-grandchildren. The work I had put into the deal began to take its toll, exhaustion set in, and I began to feel close to a breakdown. I started to resent my job, feeling increasingly lonely and trapped in a company with shareholders that I had to serve for the next few years. I blamed colleagues unfairly, thinking they had not had to work as hard as I had for the deal. I was feeling guilty for failing to be a good wife, struggling with motherhood and overwhelming tiredness, and giving no support to my friends or wider family. But while my manic drive and determination impoverished me personally, the business became more and more successful as we bought another company and increased our profits to over £1 million.

I struggled on, not knowing where to turn for help. I lacked a real mentor, did not want to admit the extent of my problems to friends or family and had no clear spiritual guidance. I started to worry about aspects of my behaviour, such as taking detours down to the sea on my way to the office and barely remembering how I got there. I seemed to swing from intense frustration at other people's behaviour to bouts of self-pity as I failed to find any kind of balance in my life. I began to close in on myself, making it impossible for anyone to help me. Perhaps it is not surprising, then, that the news from America of Hayden and Cameron's terminal illness later in 1999 forced me to begin to confront my own situation. It was impossible for James and me not to look at our own children and realize that they ought to be our real priority, while many of the petty worries in our working lives seemed insignificant.

By Christmas 2000, Hayden had died and Cameron appeared to be close to death. We had had our extraordinary summer with her, which had been such a turning point for me. Yet I felt powerless to help from across the Atlantic Ocean. I had begun to make some changes at work to make life more manageable, but when a girlfriend mentioned the possibility of joining a pilgrimage to a place called Medjugorje in Bosnia as a way to help me with my problems, I found myself accepting. I was lucky to be travelling with a close friend, Fi, who was very worried about her sister's breast cancer and had a conviction that prayer was needed. I still wonder where the courage came from for me to take this unusual and daunting step, but at the time it seemed something I could usefully do for Cameron.

We drove through Mostar, still littered with the debris of war, and past the famous bridge, destroyed in the fighting. We saw NATO tanks and buildings burned out and scarred with holes from gun and mortar attacks. As I looked, I saw the interiors were blackened with soot, and yet there was washing hanging from the balconies. It was the very European character of the place that disturbed me most, reminding me that this was a country almost on our doorstep. Avenues of trees might have been part of the towns in the south of France, but here they led only to huge burial grounds full of the graves of children, where Muslim and Christian mothers wept together.

We met Matthew Proctor, an ex-public schoolboy who had found himself on an aid convoy to Bosnia and decided to stay to work for a charity called Miracles. I was intrigued. This was not an easy country, even with the peace accord in place. Refugees and orphans, many having lost limbs to landmines, flooded back into the area, and Roma gypsy families lived on the local rubbish dumps. Matthew told me that his father had died when he was eleven, leaving him confused and struggling with everyday life, and he went a bit astray in his teenage years. He had ended up with a good job with BT, but being made redundant had given him the chance to join an aid convoy in 1993. He was appalled by the human suffering he saw then and wanted to do something about it. He had a strong faith and was horrified at the difference

17

between life in the UK and the misery here. Since then, he has worked with people of all religious backgrounds, caring in many different ways for those that are suffering and helping them achieve independence on a one-to-one basis. Meeting someone like Matthew started to make me realize that there was so much more I could be doing to help others.

Emerging from the rubble and the tears of Mostar, nearby Medjugorje was a tranquil oasis in a beautiful landscape, barely touched by the war. We were grateful to be staying in a simple but friendly *pension* owned by Kata Sivric and her family. Although I grew up in the Protestant tradition, I had had little to do with religion for some time. This was a place where the Virgin Mary had allegedly appeared to a group of children in 1981 and now, as grown men and women, they continued to have apparitions and pass on her words. I certainly had not thought much about the role of Mary – especially as she is celebrated at Medjugorje, with her messages of inner peace through forgiveness and prayer. But whether you believe in the apparitions or not, the comfort that the thousands of pilgrims draw from this place is an inescapable fact, as are the positive benefits that have come about for so many as the result of the belief.

The village is full of remarkable charitable enterprises to help the orphans of war, the poverty-stricken and even drug addicts from all over the world, for whom there are recovery programmes. Everywhere we went, we witnessed a common phenomenon – men, women and children glowing, serene and joyful, suffused with a feeling I longed to have. There was a brotherhood and sisterhood among all the visitors – your past life, your achievements (or lack of them), your social background; all seemed to be of no importance.

On Sunday 22 April 2001, reflecting on Cameron's impending death, I found myself walking with my fellow pilgrims into the Cenacolo Community, and my own life was turned upside down. An Italian nun, Sister Elvira, founded the community to help drug addicts recover with a simple life of work, friendship and prayer. In a tiny chapel I heard the testimony of a young, well-dressed, ex-college student from Boston called Sean (his story appears in Chapter 11) and felt that he was speaking to me alone. His link to the city on the other side of the world where Cameron was dying seemed extraordinary to me. Tears streamed down my face as he told the story of his battle with his addictions which had brought him close to death, and how meaningless his secular and materialistic life seemed in comparison with the joy he felt now. He spoke of how we are all 'called' to this place for a reason, and I knew immediately that it was time for me to think about my future. I longed to feel some of the joy that was so visible on his face and to find a way to live a more meaningful life. I was intrigued by his own turning point and inspired by his story of transformation. Having spent many years living behind the mask of a confident businesswoman, it was astonishing for me to see a man like Sean reveal his vulnerabilities. I realized too how easily I had judged those weaknesses and was determined to stop ignoring those in need.

The next morning, our group climbed Cross Mountain, which marked another important stage in my journey. An arduous walk over rocks and cliffs, the route follows the traditional Christian Stations of the Cross, leading to a 9-metre-high crucifix, built by the villagers in the 1930s, on the mountain summit. As we climbed, I began to understand the emphasis on Mary's role as the mother of Jesus, and the sacrifice she had made as she watched and accepted her son's agonizing death for the sake of others. As we walked, I thought of my friend Blyth watching her beautiful daughter Cameron's life come to an end, and of Hayden's mother Aliey, suffering the loss of her son. I felt the agony of their sorrow, but as I wrote to the Lord family at the time in the hope it would give them some comfort, 'I felt more than ever that the babies' suffering had a purpose' – in just the way that Mary's had. I knew too that I had somehow to be part of that purpose and that I was being given a second chance to do something that would honour the children's lives.

The service of Adoration held in the main church late that night spoke again of our unique calling and the need for us to forgive ourselves and others, to rid ourselves of any bitterness in our lives if we were going to move forward with peace in our hearts. We all left with a sense that we could make a difference in the world if we were prepared to make a few sacrifices, but also wondering how we were going to explain many of our experiences to our friends.

I have returned to Medjugorje several times since for my benefit and to help others. Each time it feels like a great challenge to take the three flights and a long bus journey from Scotland, but I never regret it; the peace and quiet provides essential time out from a busy life and gives me a chance to reflect on the mistakes I have made and my hopes for the future. Father Edward, one of our many delightful spiritual leaders, reminds us that we are always there for a reason. He believes that we all have a deep need of God and of his love even if we can't articulate it. It is in our weak moments that we are often drawn to him, one of the many issues I am tempted to explore in other people's turning points.

Cameron died shortly after my return from that first pilgrimage, following a lovely celebration of her birthday with family and friends. Her mother, Blyth, who had so wanted to believe that she was handing Cameron over to God, received my letter telling her about my experience and my sense that her suffering had a purpose, and it reinforced all she had thought. She wrote later: 'When Cameron died I knew her Spirit went to God. Although I deeply miss the physicality of her, I feel deeply privileged to have been her mother.'

The year 2001 turned out to be one of accolades, both for me and the business. Among other prizes, I was the first woman to win the Scottish Business Achievement Award and was a Veuve Clicquot Businesswoman of the Year finalist. Both were marvellous rewards that nevertheless left me hollow inside after my recent experiences. I decided to turn for advice to people I admired and who had a spiritual understanding. Sir Tom Farmer of Kwik-Fit fame was a client of Hamilton and Inches and seemed the right kind of role model, as a successful businessman and philanthropist. I still felt I needed to continue my business life somehow and was pleased that when I met with him within a week of my return, he spoke of his own belief that helping others is morally right and also good for business. However, the most important thing he did was to introduce me to a remarkable man called John Moorhouse, who was to change my life dramatically by introducing me to people who were actually working on the ground in Scotland helping others.

It seems staggering now to think how blind I was to the real circumstances of many Scots, how easily I could swallow without question the political views of those who had absolutely no inkling of the realities of life as it is lived on poor estates. For the first time I visited forgotten places like Easterhouse, a part of Glasgow where so many families suffer third-generation unemployment and a very poor life expectancy. I remember my friend Stuart Miller driving me past a run-down building, partly burned down and surrounded by barbed wire. I assumed it was some kind of dilapidated prison and was horrified to discover it was a functioning school. I found it hard to imagine how a young person could have any hope for the future or confidence in themselves in this environment. The more of this world I saw – the world that I had ignored on my own doorstep for so long but one that even brought back memories of the broken town of Mostar – the more determined I became to do something significant to help.

That summer, I spent some time on the Isle of Skye and met young people involved with Columba 1400, a charity founded by Norman Drummond that realizes the potential of those who come from the toughest realities. The stories I heard of abuse, of loneliness and depression, of children who come out of care at the age of sixteen and are no longer considered anyone's responsibility, were horrifying. I was humbled and ashamed that they appeared to admire my success in the business world without resenting me. Their lack of self-pity and passionate desire to make a difference in their communities was inspirational: I wanted to find a way to help them achieve that aim and improve their own chances in life.

Soon after, I sat with Cameron and Hayden's parents, told them all I'd seen, and asked for their advice as experienced leaders in the charity world in the US. They mentioned AmeriCorps, a volunteering organization founded by President Clinton – and an idea was born for a radical new volunteer service for young people, offering full-time placements and living expenses; a two-way street where energetic people, often from disadvantaged backgrounds, learn vital skills and self-confidence, skills that they then use to transform the work of under-resourced charities.

But before I could think of developing the idea, I had to decide what to do about my working life. Filled with new-found enthusiasm to make a difference, I was struggling to stay interested in the world of jewellery. My involvement with Columba 1400 was absorbing much of my attention and was giving me a great sense of fulfilment. We were at a stage in our business when we might have considered a sale, which would realize some capital for all the shareholders. This had plenty of appeal but could have meant losing the hard-won independence of the business. It might also have tied me in for several more years, which was something I needed to face. Was I prepared to make the leap that would see me give up my well-paid working life and career for an unknown future? I turned to my family and my fellow pilgrim, Fi, who reminded me of my experience in Medjugorje and my determination for it to lead to something. I knew my family really needed more of my time and wanted to see me happier again.

By late October 2002, I decided to tell my colleagues that I intended to leave the company that we had rebuilt together. It seems astonishing now that I thought they might be pleased. I was so busy moving in a new direction that I had completely failed to think about the effect my decision, as the major shareholder, would have on others. I had failed to share enough of my journey with them, to help them understand why I felt the way I did. As a result, the next few months were some of the hardest of my life, as close relationships were badly affected by legal wrangling. I am not proud of my role in the situation, and it took some time to rebuild the relationships. There were times when I barely had the courage to go on, but this time I had the new-found strength of my faith to fall back on and the support of my husband, who longed to see the situation that was causing me so much unhappiness brought to an end. Looking back, the difficulties had the advantage of making it easier for me to walk away from the business without too much regret. I remember hosting my leaving party and feeling sadness but also a great deal of excitement for the future.

The quiet life did not last long. After a short time off, I accepted a non-executive director role at LloydsTSB Scotland on the advice of Sir Tom Farmer, who felt I should keep my hand in the business world. Meanwhile, at the request of Scotland's First Minister, I put a team together to start building the volunteering organization that would be launched as ProjectScotland on 11 May 2004, one of the many ripple effects from the death of Cameron just three years before. By 2008, 2,000 young Scots had done more than 2 million volunteering hours for Scotland's communities, and I could feel really proud of that achievement when we received the Scottish Social Entrepreneur of the Year Award for our work.

Alongside this new direction in my working life, I realized that I had many issues I needed to resolve if I was to find the joy that I had seen in Sean's face that day in Medjugorje. One of the best decisions I made was to take part in the Hoffman Process, an intensive residential course of personal discovery and development. After all the challenges of leaving my business, I arrived for the week feeling nervous and scared. A fellow graduate recalled perceiving me on that first day as 'posh, confident and clever but also quiet, tense, trapped, frightened and unsure'. By the time I left, I had shaken off that confident mask and protective shell I had worn for so many years of my life and was described as 'smiling, joyful, relaxed, confident and happy'. All the disappointments and shame I felt for past mistakes had gone. Coming to terms with my vulnerabilities and becoming aware of my weaknesses, I could move on without regret for the past, really appreciating all that I have in my life. Finding a sensible balance between working life and family life is still a struggle, but at least I am aware of it and know the steps to take to make things better. A quote from one of my favourite books, *Gift from the Sea*, by Anne Morrow Lindbergh, speaks to my personal transformation: 'When one is a stranger to oneself, then one is estranged from others too. If one is out of touch with oneself, then one cannot touch others.'

Since that day at Cenacolo when I heard Sean speak, I have tried to be a greater support to friends and family. A few years later, in 2003, a close friend lost her young son, Dougie, to cancer. Her faith was severely challenged, but she agreed that three of us would meet and try to pray with her every week. We eventually decided to ask others to join us and to do our own Alpha course, which gave us a structure to explore our faith. It provided a great deal of clarity for me and a chance for us to try to make more sense of the loss of these children we had known. We have continued to meet as a group of women for many years, and it is an essential part of my life today as I try to balance and nurture my physical, emotional and spiritual lives, not always with great success. I take such pleasure now in my friendships and my relationship with my children. If I need any reminder of the need for change in my life, I can look at two notes I keep with me: the first from my young son in my business days, who once wrote, 'I love you so much that I want you to stai off wrck [sic],' and the second, more recently, from my daughter, who told me very movingly in a card that I was 'the best mum, always there for me'. Nothing is more important to me now than the simple pleasures of family life.

I asked all those I interviewed about their turning points for the epitaph they would like for themselves. I was inspired by my grandmother's funeral many years before, when we were all reminded of how much she was loved as a mother, grandmother, sister and friend. I stood there wondering whether being remembered as 'Businesswoman of the Year' was what I wanted to see on my headstone. What on earth would that say about me? Like everyone, I wanted to be loved and remembered for my relationships and for what I did for others. After Cameron died, her father sent me this poem, Raymond Carver's 'Late Fragment':

And did you get what
you wanted from this life,
even so?
I did.
And what did you want?
To call myself beloved, to feel myself
beloved on the earth.

I am so grateful that knowing Cameron and Hayden has given me the chance to share in a small way their experience of being beloved, to be able to make a difference in people's lives and feel the gift of joy that comes from that. I was able to see the moment of Cameron's passing as a turning point for me – a second chance at life. I am lucky to have a remarkable family to inspire and support me, all committed to improving the lives of others through their charitable projects. Everywhere I go, I meet people who have faced challenging moments in their lives, and so often these do become turning points, a chance to take a different road. I became fascinated with this idea and set out to discover more.

What is a turning point – a dramatic bolt from the heavens or a sense of unease that life lacks meaningful purpose, resulting in a gentle change of course? Why do some people respond to a crisis in a positive way, while others can appear to lose their joy in living – is it to do with character or the nature of what they have suffered? Is faith and service to others important? There seem to be as many varieties of turning point as there are people. I hope these stories will inspire those who read them to respond to life with similar courage.

2

GORDON BROWN

My turning point was the result of a personal tragedy that happened to close friends of mine. For Gordon and Sarah Brown, it was very different. They had to cope with the tragic death of their own baby daughter Jennifer and in the full spotlight of the media.

I have known Gordon Brown for a while, having met him through his wife, Sarah. We share a Fife address, and Sarah and I have had various charity interests in common. When Gordon became Prime Minister, he asked me, as a social entrepreneur, to join his Council for Social Action, which meets regularly at Downing Street. It has been fascinating to work with a group of remarkable individuals on some of the key social issues that are affecting Britain today.

I have always been intrigued by Gordon. Like many people, I had an image of him gained through the media that was often at odds with what he actually did. He appeared to be an ambitious, intellectual man without the amenable persona that Tony Blair presented. However, once I had met him, my opinion changed. At a dinner at his Fife home, I discovered a very charming and entertaining host, someone who was easy to talk to and who clearly enjoyed the company of women. He was particularly warm in his praise of my mother-in-law, Princess Alexandra, appreciating the quiet way she has served her country for so many years, and when my father-in-law, Sir Angus Ogilvy, died of cancer in 2004, he was one of the first to send a handwritten note to my husband. Since then I have seen many examples of his loyalty to his friends and his love of his family and country. Like many of my interviewees, he believes in serving others, and I hoped to discover why that was so important to him.

I was aware of the impact the loss of their daughter Jennifer had had on both Gordon and Sarah and was keen to understand how that tragic turning point had affected his political life and how it had changed him. We met in September 2006 at his home in Scotland, a comfortable Victorian house with all the usual chaos of a family with two small children. Any nerves I had about the impending conversation were easily forgotten as his irresistibly cute son John showed me his train set, delighted to have his father to play with him.

I knew that I was lucky to be there at all. Gordon has never talked willingly in public about this very private time in his life. During other interviews, unplanned discussions about his personal life or work for charity have led to painful exchanges about Jennifer. He had been horrified by the ensuing media responses, with their mix of sensational headlines about his 'heartache' and cynical comments about his motivation. I wondered how I would persuade him to open up to me. Naturally, it helped that I was not a journalist and that this was a very informal meeting in the midst of family life. It was also important that we had common ground. He knew that setting up ProjectScotland, an organization he greatly admires and even mentioned in his speech at a party conference, had been my response to the loss of two small children. It was not surprising that he began our conversation by asking more about that experience.

When I told him more about the deaths of Cameron and Hayden Lord and passed him their photograph, a small tear fell from his eye and became trapped in a fold of skin beneath it. Throughout our discussion, this droplet remained where it was, occasionally catching the sunlight and telling me more about him than almost anything else he said that day. Before long, Gordon had started to tell me more about the shattering loss of his daughter Jennifer, who was born two months prematurely and died of a brain haemorrhage when she was only ten days old. Her picture sat on the table between us, a tiny two-pound spark of life almost dwarfed by tubes and medical equipment. Rather than concentrate on the sorrow, I asked Gordon how he'd felt when she was born. At times, he would take a deep breath or fall silent, struggling for the right way to talk about this painful subject.

'I was overjoyed. The happiness of seeing a first child, a daughter, born is something that you just cannot describe, even [when it takes place] in difficult circumstances. It was particularly difficult because she was born just after Christmas, a lot earlier than we had expected. She was so incredibly small – two pounds – and fragile in an incubator. But because we were surrounded in this children's unit by other small babies in incubators, and even though Sarah was very unwell, I still thought everything would work out fine. I gave an interview standing in front of the cameras... saying just how happy I was, with no idea of the problems ahead. We were accepting people's congratulations, and toys and clothes were arriving.

'It took days before I had to come to terms with the fact that there was something wrong. We were still believing that, although our baby was very small, she was going to grow and she was going to develop. And Sarah was producing milk for her and everything else, so it was the shock of finding after a few days that you were looking at a beautiful baby that seemed untouched by any illness or sickness or tragedy, and then finding that there was something so fundamentally wrong that there was nothing that could be done. It was a terrible, terrible shock.

'People started saying that she wasn't responding properly, and that she had to move from the hospital in Kirkcaldy to the Royal Infirmary in Edinburgh in order to see all the specialist doctors. But we still thought there was a great deal of hope. We knew there was an issue about how she wasn't growing, but she was still able to respond to us talking to her, showing us that she knew we were there. So we still thought things would work out, but that it just might take her longer to flourish.

'But by the Friday night I'd started to work it out, and draw my own conclusion that there was no hope, something Sarah and I had been trying to avoid. It wasn't anything anyone said. I just started to know that she wasn't responding and therefore it couldn't go forward, it would always go backwards. And that was the most terrible, terrible moment.

'I left the hospital and came home. I called a doctor friend and told him everything, saying that I thought there was no chance. He said I would have to talk to the surgeon tomorrow, but I might have to face up to it. Then the doctor told us on the Saturday that there was absolutely no hope whatsoever, so all we could do was to sit with her for twenty-four hours a day, sleeping in the hospital. We didn't realize it would be such a short period. Although we had reached the conclusion that she wouldn't live, you think maybe you've got more days. We just had to keep going for Jennifer, and I had to keep going for Sarah.'

There was nothing cautious about his words now. Gordon seemed to have forgotten there was a microphone between us, and as he spoke the tears would well up frequently in his eyes. He spoke softly when he described the awful pain he had endured and seemed lost in the memories of that time. He has a very expressive face, and his sorrow was clearly visible. He mentioned how important it had been to keep going for his wife's sake – but I sensed that she had also been key to keeping him together through that time.

'Sarah may have known all along that things were more difficult. As the mother feeding her and just understanding more about how babies should grow, she was probably more aware than I was. But it was an incredible shock to me, because I'd been elated about being a father. I realized there were problems, but I'd always thought that they were soluble and I just thought it was just a matter of time before we would see the baby grow and gain strength. You would never have been able to tell by looking at Jennifer that there was anything at all wrong.

'Anyway, we just knew that it was all ebbing away, and she was baptized on the Sunday at her cot by our local minister, Sheila Munro. And that's one of the photographs we have. There was nursing help to avoid pain and suffering for the baby. So once they'd done that, we knew it meant she would die that day. She died on the Monday at five o'clock.

'And then we had to leave the hospital. We actually didn't want to leave; it's one of those things when your baby or mother or father dies – you don't want to leave, but you have to. I think someone stole a photograph of us as we were trying to leave very privately. And it was very difficult to come home. In the past, when a baby died at ten days old, there wouldn't have been a funeral, but we thought it right to have one. I also had to tell my mother – she never saw the baby alive, and my brother Andrew had arrived just too late, too.'

I reminded Gordon of the words spoken by his brother John at the funeral: '[She] brought great joy: joy so deep, a love so immediate and intense, that the anxiety, the loss that followed, are almost unbearable. So for Sarah and Gordon their lives were transformed… twice over: first as they wept tears of happiness and then of sorrow.'

Seeking to leave behind the painful memories associated with the loss, I asked him to talk about the impact of Jennifer's short life. Did he feel any sense of purpose could be found in its ending? He sat up in his seat, his body language changed, and he appeared to have turned a corner as he spoke, showing his determined side.

'It certainly made you aware of time, because we only had ten days and you can almost remember every moment of those ten days. It makes you aware that you must never waste your time. As a parent, you can achieve a great deal in ten days, you know – you feel the baby knew that love surrounded her; you feel that she recognized our voices and our touch, and we were able to hold her hand. But I think you keep asking, "What is the bigger thing? What is the purpose? What has actually happened here? And why us?" I couldn't listen to music for six months. I went back to Parliament, but it was the last place I wanted to be at that time. I had no interest in what I regarded as minor issues. Your view of what is important changes fundamentally.

'I believe, no matter in what circumstances a child is brought into this world, it should have a decent start, but major medical barriers have got to be overcome. We don't know enough about what happened to Jennifer and other babies. More research has to be done. You want to do everything you can to eliminate avoidable pain and unnecessary suffering. And for many people, the loss and pain can be avoided. You can make a difference quickly, too. With the new focus on healthcare for young children and on vaccination, we're talking about thousands, perhaps hundreds of thousands of families being able to avoid the suffering that any parent goes through when a child just dies.

'For me, there was no obvious "turning point" moment. But I think it was my immediate reaction that something good had to come from losing Jennifer; we had to think what we could do that would make a difference. It might explain what had happened to us and make sure that small life would not have been lived in vain. The decision to do something was made during the days between her death and funeral at home here in Scotland. And then it was developed into something more solid later, when Sarah started to receive so many letters from people who'd shared the same experience.

'While there are organizations that give assistance in terms of advice, one thing we noticed was that there's just not enough research going into why these tragedies happen. So the Jennifer Brown Research Fund which we set up, is looking at new ways of helping both pregnant mothers and newborn babies. Sarah has done a remarkable job setting up a number of research projects, all of which are yielding results now, and which have been pretty well financed by both local people here and by national charities. Many children and community groups have been giving small but very important amounts of money to the project.

'In global terms, there are 6 million children born every year who should be alive but for medicine, drugs and the right treatment. Our research projects can have a huge influence on Africa and the developing world. That's what I mean when I say my whole philosophy has changed as a result of what happened to Jennifer.

'I mean, if you can't help one child, then don't try to say you can help millions of children. You have got to be able to do both. You start by showing you can make one child better, and then you show that you can help hundreds of thousands of children. I have visited all these different countries in Africa, and the focus of these trips has often been what we can do for children. I want the research that is being done in Britain to be available round the world, so we've got to find a means by which that research is properly shared. I've launched an education initiative with other action groups. I think we can probably be the first generation in history to make it possible for every child to have schooling.

'We are working on a malaria vaccine, as 2 million children die each year from malaria – again, completely avoidable. We've put huge amounts of money into vaccination for children, too. And as a result of the project we've been involved in with Bill Gates and GAVI [The Global Alliance for Vaccines and

Immunization], we think 5 million deaths can be avoided over the next ten to fifteen years. It's appalling to see the waste of life simply due to there being no vaccine or no mosquito nets for families. This is not a problem of science or medicine; this is a problem of making the results of good science and good medicine available to more people. You're not looking for a technological breakthrough; you're simply looking for the capacity to give people either drugs or treatment or vaccination. Sometimes it's just about helping mothers to know about some of the modern ways in which childbirth can be a lot easier.

'Jennifer did live for a purpose if what she was to us can also make a difference to people's lives. Everything Sarah and I do now is founded on this idea. We can show that even though she didn't live, the goodness she represented is carried on in a meaningful way. I said to Sarah at the time that nothing would be exactly as it was before, and that I didn't think we could live without doing something that made what happened to us meaningful.'

I wondered exactly what Gordon understood by 'meaningful' – if perhaps it indicated a religious outlook as well as a political one. With a politician's acumen, he didn't exactly deny it: 'If we have been helped in doing that, if that purpose has been given to us, then I do have a faith that that's what's happened.'

'Other priorities change. I had never visited hospitals in my life apart from the time I had that succession of eye operations as a student, and I never wanted to go back. Now I want to help the hospitals in my constituency, and I want to be involved with them. I've travelled the world as well, to try to help get this vaccination initiative moving for children, because I don't want parents to go through what we went through.'

As he mixed talk of parenthood and global issues, I had the clearest possible picture of Gordon's inherent conflict. He is a devoted family man, a man changed forever by the loss of a newborn daughter, yet he would soon become Prime Minister, a tireless campaigner on a world stage, an active force for change. I wondered whether lobbying for child health, as well as being the result of his bereavement, was also his way of reconciling the difference between the two Gordons. He admitted that it was a daily struggle.

'I think if we'd had our children when we were very young, we would probably have been more cavalier about it. Certainly if we'd had our children without losing Jennifer, we would have been a lot more easy-going about our responsibilities. Now I think everything is so precious you want to freeze-frame some times and have this moment go on forever; these different stages of a child's life are just unrepeatable and just so precious. Jennifer would have been going to school by now. You think what you would have been doing, but you have to come to terms with the fact that she won't and just look at your new priorities.'

You don't reach middle age, and you certainly don't reach middle age in British political life, without becoming acquainted with untimely death – the death of parents, friends, colleagues – but the death of a child you had never come to know must be an entirely different kind of sorrow. Where did the crucial difference lie?

'I remember it was a terrible shock when my father died – he just collapsed and died from a stroke, and I'd been talking to him the night before. I felt that we were always rushing, always in a hurry and that I didn't give him enough time, even in the last conversation we had. He was an incredible influence on my life, a sort of a moral compass. I think we said at my father's funeral that most people need a moral compass, but for us as brothers and his sons, he was our compass. It wasn't theology, it was more a sense of what was the right thing to do. It doesn't leave you, but obviously you miss the direct influence. With my mother, we were with her for many weeks when she wasn't well, and we were able to say things to her that we were never able to say to my father, and I think that does make a difference. But it's quite difficult when, in a succession of a few years, your father, your daughter and your mother go. It leaves such a big void.

'But at least with my mother and father, they had reached a point in their lives where death was natural. It's just incomprehensible that a young child of ten days should go. I think religion is about trying to understand what is essentially unknowable. And you do get an understanding of what makes sense, but it takes a lot of time.'

A lot of pain and rage, I prompted, thinking of the various reactions to deaths that I'd seen. But Gordon didn't quite agree.

'I don't think we were ever angry. You can have a whole bewildering range of emotions about pointlessness: "Why us?" which I suppose is a form of anger. But I think we've been helped in some way. I can't explain exactly how, but we've been helped in finding a more meaningful purpose to the rest of our lives.

'I've had other turning points in my life, because when I was sixteen I almost went blind [due to a sporting injury]. I decided then that if I couldn't play football or rugby, and I was being prevented from having the normal teenage years, then there had to be a reason. There had to be something that I was going to do that was useful. I decided I wasn't going to be a lecturer as I'd planned. I was going to do something about public service, although some people don't think that politics is public service.'

I was touched by this image of an earnest sixteen-year-old, coping with the deadening prospect of blindness by deciding to devote himself to politics. Teenage years can be a time of rebellion and selfishness, but Gordon's words reminded me that it's also often an age of deeply felt convictions, passionate views and concern for humanity, just as I see in the young people who volunteer for ProjectScotland. I realized that the roots of Gordon's concern for fairness and social justice ran deep. But even so, what made him – as a sixteen-year-old, and later on after the death of Jennifer – seek a purpose in what had happened, seek to turn loss into growth? To me it felt quite a religious outlook – one perhaps influenced by his Church of Scotland minister father.

'I think it's biblical, actually. You go to church every Sunday, go to Sunday School and grow up in the kind of home I grew up in, and you know the parable of the good Samaritan: "don't walk by on the other side" and phrases like "do as you would be done by", "suffer the little children" and "blessed are the poor". Probably the first sound bites in history, aren't they?

'When my father was a minister, you had all these people coming to our house asking for help, and he never turned anybody away. If people wanted help, he would give them something. I remember him explaining to me what unemployment was. I remember one day 500 people losing their jobs in a place just up the road from where we stayed. And when these things are explained to you, there is a sense of what is fair. It does grow based on the experiences you see around you, but I think it starts from an idea that people should be treated fairly.

'Some people say that in this combination of Scottish Enlightenment philosophy and Scottish religion is this idea of justice. If you look back on the Scottish Enlightenment and at the philosophers David Hume, Adam Smith and right through that period, what they were trying to do was to explain moral sense. My home town of Kirkcaldy, where Adam Smith wrote his *Wealth of Nations*, was a trading centre. So he could see how wealth could be created by trade between different countries, but he was actually more interested, as I am, in what he called the "moral sense". You see, the great feature of the Industrial Revolution years in Scotland and England, actually, is that at the same time as this dramatic economic development was taking place, there was also this extraordinary growth of charitable activity and philanthropy and desire for self-improvement.

There was a notion of a moral sense, a light in man, whatever you call it, the better angels of our nature. That moral sense includes a sense of what is fair. Empathy towards other people.

'Every generation has got to find its own answers to these questions. We moved to a society that was built around the individual, but we are returning now to a huge growth of social enterprise, a huge interest in community action. People [are] understanding that there are limits, both to what markets can do and what states can do, and that there's this range of contributions that people can make, just by acting as individuals in their communities. It's almost a philosophical shift over the last twenty years – people searching for forms of community, even in a fast-changing world, where they acknowledge their responsibilities to each other and find a way of discharging them. And it does arise, I think, from that moral sense. Every religion has at the centre of it this idea of people's responsibility to others. Whether you look at the Qur'an, or the sayings of the Buddha, or Jewish texts, they're all suggesting that you do to others as you would be done by yourself. That is the heart of this moral sense. I think we all have it, and I think you see it in children as they grow up. There are all sorts of contradictory pressures upon them, but there remains this sense of fairness. But it also depends on the circumstances of the particular community or country. You know, I grew up in a town where there were so many voluntary and community organizations – it's often difficult to forget that that wasn't true of many other areas.'

I was conscious that there was a lot of movement in the Brown household, and that I'd taken up a great deal of Gordon's time already. But I was intrigued by the idea of moral sense as the core of his character. I wondered whether it was how he'd choose to be remembered, whether there was something he wanted to see on his tombstone.

'Service, I think; it's the only thing we can do. Martin Luther King said that everybody can be great because everybody can serve, and therefore there is no distinction between people in positions of power or those who are relatively powerless. But we can all achieve something. My family used to say you will leave your mark one way or another. You can leave it for good or for ill and you've got that choice. You have to keep asking if you're actually making a difference – if you're not, then you should do something else.'

As I prepared to leave, it struck me how very little resemblance the man I'd been talking to bore to the mythical figure often presented in the media. But I could also see how that image came about. Gordon's reluctance to speak so openly in the way he had to me made it harder for people outside his immediate circle to know or understand him – and in the absence of understanding, there was this very misleading image. Perhaps that was how he saw it, too?

'I think it's partly about politics, isn't it? Politics is seen by so many people as self-serving. People may start out with good motives but then are thought to be just out for themselves. But it's also partly because I've come from a background which is probably very similar to yours; that is, reserved. You don't actually like talking about yourself, and you feel it's imposing on other people to talk about yourself. I do understand, though, that if you're in public life, people need to know who you are. And you've got a responsibility to explain why you're doing what you're doing. I will try to do that, but, you know, it's a challenge. It's probably an opportunity, but you might say it hasn't been properly done so far. But one of the other things about being a Member of Parliament in the constituency where I grew up and went to school is that I know large numbers of people. People I was at school with, people I played football with. And I keep meeting those friends again – and I do get a sense that there is hope, and an understanding of the contribution that people are trying to make in public life.

'I think all of us, in any party, are, to some extent, a victim of the conflict-ridden atmosphere of the House of Commons, which doesn't yield understanding as much as it should. I think we should learn from that and try to be a bit humbler. We will see a greater focus on character rather than celebrity in the years to come. In the same way that we're describing these movements that are encouraging people to play a bigger part in their communities, it is also bringing back a concern for the profound rather than the superficial, an interest in the spiritual rather than the material – and, equally, a sense that people should be known not for what they say they are, but for what they *really* are.'

As our conversation ended, I felt profoundly moved and hoped that it had somehow helped him to be able to talk about Jennifer and what really mattered to him at such a difficult time. It was a privilege to have had this insight into a man of extraordinary character and frustrating that few people get to see this side of him. Naturally, different political views will create a barrier, and as a public figure there will always be a difference between what people think of you and what you are and do.

It is clear that Jennifer's death was a turning point that had led to a new focus for Gordon as a man as well as a future Prime Minister, a new way of looking at life. At the same time, I believe it was always in Gordon's character to find a meaning in the tragedy, to convert sadness into action on others' behalf, just as he'd decided to do when he was sixteen.

It is also obvious that the people who matter most to him – his wife Sarah and his own family – play a crucial role in Gordon's life. I sensed that he has a deep faith, which underpins his philosophy of life. He is immensely proud of Sarah's achievements with the Jennifer Brown Research Fund and PiggyBankKids, organizations that have a significant impact and that were founded as a direct result of the loss of their baby daughter, an impressive response to a very difficult time. Jennifer Brown may have lived for only a handful of days, but her short time on earth has had a powerful impact on babies and children all over the world.

3

CLIVE STAFFORD SMITH

The first time I heard the well-known death row lawyer Clive Stafford Smith was on *Desert Island Discs* on BBC Radio 4 one Friday morning. Several things drew my attention that day: he had lived as a child in Newmarket near where I grew up; he had been at Radley College, a boys' boarding school where I attended school dances; and he chose some of my favourite songs on the programme, from 'Dancing Queen' by Abba to 'Spem in Alium' by the choir of King's College, Cambridge. He was only five years older than me, but clearly his life had gone in a very different direction.

While I had gone to St Andrews University, found a career in marketing and business and lived a fairly conventional life, he had headed for America and became a lawyer on death row. He seemed to have developed a social conscience at an early age, something he shared with Gordon Brown. I was intrigued by the path he took and glad to hear the presenter Sue Lawley ask him why he had made that choice and whether there had been an obvious turning point in his life. In response, he referred to writing an essay at school on capital punishment and his shock that the death penalty still existed. I felt certain there must be more to it than that.

Clive now lives in Dorset with his English wife, Emily, and son, Wilfred, but we met at the London offices of Reprieve, a charity he founded which uses the law to enforce the human rights of prisoners from death row to Guantanamo Bay. Clive is a tall man with a strong presence, laid-back charm and a disarming smile. He didn't appear to care too much about his wardrobe but had a casual trendiness about him in the way he dressed. Even when seated he seemed full of energy, optimism and enthusiasm. He was quite open and happy to talk about anything and it was obvious that he would find it easy to build up trust with his clients. We met at a time when his father was gravely ill and close to death, and he had spent several hours at his bedside the night before. Clive found it quite hard to talk about him and his illness but was happy to talk about the challenges of his childhood.

'I had a very privileged childhood in contrast to many others. I grew up on a horse stud farm in Newmarket and I think its claim to fame was that it had more horse boxes than any other stud farm. My grandparents had inherited it and eventually it went to my father. My family were sort of *nouveau riche* before they became *nouveau pauvre* again when it went bankrupt. It was an amazing place, something that I think no private individual should have the right to monopolize. Not surprisingly, I went to posh schools and had in many ways an incredibly privileged background. I was happy at school even though I don't approve of places like that now.

'However, there was more to it. My dad was bipolar. This is a manic depressive illness and it was a big factor in the bankruptcy of our farm and in my childhood experience. As a child, strange things would happen. For example, when I was about seven, he took us into the living room and said, "Today you have to choose between me and your mother, and if you choose your mother, I'll never talk to you again"; another time that year he came up to me and said, "Here's £200; go live somewhere else. You're old enough to live on your own, but if you want to stay you can pay us rent," and all sorts of things like that. It was not often that he was completely normal although my dad tended to be more manic than depressed. He had been diagnosed the year I was born but didn't take the medication so it was never controlled. My parents split up when I was eleven, and the stud farm went bankrupt soon after. It was only some years later that I realized my father wasn't bad, but mentally ill. I knew I had a difficult father but it was particularly painful for my mother and more so for my older brother and sister who were less naïve than I was. My mother was a saint, putting up with my father for a long time and protecting us.

'I remember that time very clearly. My sister was very upset by the bankruptcy because I think she would have loved to work with horses as a career, but I always had a sense that there was something wrong with it all. I used to go around this enormous 365-acre idyll, and it was all our family's and no one else got to go there and that just struck me as very unfair and such a waste. I have always had a total inability to remember negative things just like my mother does so perhaps it was not surprising that I saw the bankruptcy in a positive way. I was away at school, but my dad ended up leaving the country to live in Spain for fifteen years so that was very hard for my mum. I think he probably had to and at that time there was no extradition treaty. I only saw him two or three times in that whole period.

'When I think about my involvement in fighting the death penalty, I talk about an essay I wrote on capital punishment at school, but it wasn't just one thing that started me off; I remember lots of little incidents. It was a kind of evolution rather than a road to Damascus moment. The earliest one I remember is from my prep school where I saw this picture of Joan of Arc getting burned at the stake and it just struck me as profoundly unfair. They make it out as the "glorious British victory" against the perfidious French, but she looked like my sister, and the idea that we were torturing her at the stake was just profoundly wrong. I do remember being at Radley, writing a history paper about the death penalty and being so surprised that the Americans were still killing each other. That was when I remember really deciding I'd better go and do something about it.

'My brother was at Cambridge University and my mother worked there, so although it would have seemed obvious for me to follow them, it was the last thing I wanted to do. I wanted to get to America to get away from all that. I ended up getting a Morehead Scholarship to study politics at the University of North Carolina at Chapel Hill, which I could apply for from Radley. It was an amazing programme there – I can't say it was academically challenging, but they had all sorts of other things such as their own radio programmes and newspapers and TV stations, and the scholarship process paid for whatever you wanted to do in the summer.

'The first summer, I went to work with the Los Angeles Sheriff's Department and found myself watching some tremendously corrupt cops in action. I am ashamed that I remember being taught how to lie on a polygraph test by thinking erotic thoughts as I did my baseline questions, but then I also saw some horrible things such as some guy getting killed by the cops. I remember I was having a drink with one of them and we were having a big argument about the death penalty, so he told me I should go work for those "communists in Atlanta", which of course I did.

'I ended up working for a guy who had given up a lot to represent people on death row. My job at the time was to visit those people and it was fascinating, absolutely intriguing for some incredibly naïve British public schoolboy to be going in every day for eight hours, talking to these men. You think, "Oh my God, what am I going to talk to these guys about?" I have this terribly privileged background and they're sitting underneath the electric chair that will take their lives. Once a week they would test the electricity and all the lights would dim and all this ghastly stuff. It really was an amazing experience.

'There were lots of things that really struck me about death row. What was really odd was that we were in America, the richest country in the world, but if you are on death row, you have no right to a lawyer. These guys were meant to represent themselves, and I remember a guy called Johnny who was one of *thirty* children, and no one in his family had visited him for the entire time he'd been on death row. I was the first person who had come to see him and he was mentally disabled – he couldn't write his own name and he was meant to represent himself. It was just obscene.

'The other thing that strikes you is that although almost everyone who's ever come to work in our office in America has favoured prison when they got there, hardly anyone has favoured it when they've left as a way to deal with society's problems. I don't think anyone should go to prison. If you think of the people you love most, you can't ever imagine sending them to prison, so you only do it to people you don't know. People can be seriously mentally ill and they need serious help but that doesn't mean prison. If they're a danger to themselves or others then yes, we need to help them, but they don't choose to do that; I mean it's crazy to think that someone wants to be mentally ill.

'We all have stereotypes about people in prison, and yet I met all these people who were fascinating and really nice and we did nothing except sit around and talk all day, except when I was running around dealing with appeals. One guy learned all this Shakespeare, and when the guards gave him trouble he would turn round and quote lines at them, which really bugged them, although in general this prison was run by very decent people.

'I had been planning to be a journalist as I thought that was going to be the way to change people's lives but I soon realized after these visits that I needed to get a law degree so I went to Columbia Law School for three years. I focused entirely on the work I wanted to do on death row even though most students there were aiming for well-paid jobs on Wall Street. Then I went to work with the Southern Centre for Human Rights in

Atlanta, having first qualified at the Louisiana Bar. The early years were a bit crazy as I hardly had any idea what I was doing. Fortunately, we used to win all the time, but I should barely have been allowed in court. I was insane, I'm sure, but I knew I had to do it and the alternative for those on death row was so dire.

'Fortunately I have only lost death penalty cases three times in my life. The first time was in 1987 when I was twenty-seven and very naïve, probably too young to really take it on board. When you have an execution they have the jury come back in and sentence someone to death, and when those twelve people that you were trying to persuade enter the room and say, "That person over there..." who you like, "is so disgusting that we want to kill him", that's actually the greatest failure I think one could possibly have; I know of nothing else that's worse than that. This man Edward Earl Johnson had been on death row for eight years and I was involved for the last three weeks. We had the BBC there making a documentary which all made it quite surreal.

'The sad truth is that I had assumed we would win, but that three-week period was interspersed by all sorts of difficult things. My then wife and I got burgled in the middle of it so I had to go back to Atlanta, and I remember Edward writing an incredibly sweet card to my wife, apologizing for the fact that I was away trying to save his life when I should have been at home... quite incredible. Three weeks turned out to be very little time, even staying up all night for days on end, and when I look back I realize that if I knew then what I know now, Edward would be alive today. We could win cases on legal technicalities that were just bizarre.

'I remember driving up to the prison before they killed him – they were having a radio call-in show about whether he should die or not and how he should die, and there's nothing quite like the distillation of hatred when it comes round to killing somebody. Edward was a nice guy; he was an eighteen-year-old

African American kid who was indisputably innocent, and the fact that these people who never bothered to meet him or learn anything serious about his case were calling up and saying that gassing and the gas chamber is too kind for him is just obscene. That's what this is really all about for me – getting between the people who are doing the hating and the people who are the objects of the hatred.

'I remember having to go and tell Edward that he'd lost his last appeal but he never believed it. Having the TV cameras there made it all surreal, and I think it made him think that someone was going to call "cut". The warden at the prison was really decent and human and let me go all the way to the gas chamber with him, and it was only when he had been strapped down for about two minutes that he realized and said to me, "Let's get it over with." It was just horrible and it took eighteen minutes for him to die. I hated being there, but I have never had a client who didn't want me to; you've got to have some friend with you.

'I always say it's not me that is suffering on death row, but the one occasion out of the six that I have been involved with that really got to me was with Nicky Ingram, a British guy. He was born in the same hospital as me in Cambridge and I'd known him for years, working on his appeals, and we were friends, sharing lots of intimate conversations. They really tortured him to death, deliberately not telling him the night before they killed him that he had a "stay" of execution following a successful appeal, even shaving his head ready for the chair so his mum would see him like that. His actual death was torture, and Nicky was never calm or collected about the process so the impact on me was huge. I left the country, went home and sat in a pub for a week.

'In spite of that, I don't feel in any sense the notion of burnout because I just can't imagine doing anything else. I think most people's jobs are incredibly boring, and the idea that you can actually go out and help people who are in such dire straits is wonderful. My reaction to what happened was very emotional and personal, but it made me even more determined that it shouldn't happen again. I remember too that when Larry [another prisoner] was executed, just before he died he said to me, "Thank you, you're the only friend who's ever stuck by me," and that's one of the incredibly empowering things about this sort of work.

'Some prisoners are religious, and by the end religion was a very good thing for Larry as he was bipolar and kept dropping his appeals. His last words were "Lord, forgive them for they know not what they do," which really p****d the Georgians off, but he was totally calm, and the idea that someone can face a torturous death like that with that sort of fortitude and calmness is important.

'As for me, I grew up going to church every day and I do find the Bible very helpful, especially when I am talking to jurors and preparing closing arguments, but I don't know if it's true. If I was designing the world, I would design it differently. I would prefer to have Mohammed rather than Jesus but just because the story is more interesting and less predictable. I do believe that everyone has a faith of some sort, and the people who pretend they are atheists just have a faith in atheism. But my faith is that I don't know and I really don't care, but there are one or two things that I believe very profoundly and they have to do with our life here. I think there's something very strange about people saving their own souls because that strikes me as being slightly selfish, and I believe we should be more concerned about the people we are dealing with here.

'After twenty-six years of working on death row, I decided to come back to England. I loved working in America but I really disliked living in America because I think, sadly, it's a very hate-filled society. I desperately want to do what I can to try and change that, but I don't want to endlessly live in a world where I'm in the "belly of the beast". It makes me a worse person when

I'm complaining about America; it doesn't have any impact on America but it has an impact on me. It's like being in a bad relationship when you just shouldn't be there.

'I set up Reprieve when I came back to England. Reprieve is about delivering justice and saving lives; it's about getting between the people who have been hated and the people doing the hating, and it's about being on the front lines. I'm all in favour of people campaigning and stuff – that's great, I'm glad they do it – but it's not for me; I want to be there with the individuals. I spend a lot of time as a lawyer at Guantanamo Bay; it was hard to get in there, but as a lawyer you do have huge power – you can force people to do things they don't want to do even if their name is George Bush. It was extraordinary to be one of the first people in there to see the prisoners, who hadn't seen anyone for three or four years and had been abused in horrible ways. We will win the battle to have the place closed in the end, but it's sad that so many people have to suffer until it ends. The awful irony is that the hatred of Muslims has transferred attention away from death row, so there have been far fewer death sentences in America since 9/11.

'It seems to me self-evident, at a level that's most basic, that if everyone is encouraged to feel good about helping other people feel good, then everyone benefits. It's silly to call people altruistic, because if we're going around doing something because it makes us feel good, then it's not, but on the other hand on a purely utilitarian level, it makes so much sense to design a society that way. We need 16 million British people doing it and then the world would be much more fun.

'I think one of the challenges is to help people to get the job they would really like to do. Most people are afraid to live, and they're afraid to live because the government and the media keeps making them afraid, and I think that our greatest challenge particularly for younger people is to teach them how to design the job they want to do. Not everyone has that privilege – and

I recognize how privileged I was – but a lot of people have the chance and yet they waste it. There are two victims of that: the people they could help, and the other is themselves. If all I had done in my life was to represent some computer firm, wouldn't that be a waste of a lifetime? Strangely enough, I'm in favour of the honours system for people who do good things in their community. I was so proud to read about this guy who got some honour for hedge-cutting in Derbyshire. You can do anything well; you can do anything in a way that helps your community and helps the people around you, and you don't have to have gone to some posh school to do that.

'If I have to think about my epitaph, I think the single thing that's most important in life is *joie de vivre*, because that's what so many people lack. If you're in pursuit of happiness, not in the selfish sense but in the self-fulfilment sense, then that's what matters, so I would want something like *joie de vivre* on my tombstone. That idea could be seen to conflict with the work I do but it is not the case. I would so much rather live in a community of my clients on death row than in an average community, because they're much more interesting, nicer people, and it's not because they're inherently that way; it's because they've had the good fortune to go through a terrible experience that's made them really look at life and value it and most people don't have that opportunity. Most people never stop in between rushing from here to there, being forced to worry about things that don't matter.

'The things people might complain about, like getting held up at gunpoint, happen to me quite routinely, and I'm so glad because it gives me the ability to talk to people who have suffered and who are wallowing in their suffering because our society teaches people to do that. It's so sad for them, you know. Most of those things that are so difficult are just great opportunities in a way, and I don't mean to be callous. Of course, some things are very hard, like my dad dying, but I am just saying that there are some tremendously positive things that come out of bad experiences. There is a silver lining to almost every dark cloud, and life is much better when you look for those as opposed to complaining.

'When I think about the key influence on my life and the way it went it probably is my dad, whose motto was always "question all authority". He was terribly anti-authoritarian, and as a result, I think I do look at the world and question things such as the death penalty. My father was a genius, but the trouble is there's a very narrow line between genius and illness, and sadly my dad crossed that line. My father was always trying to be the richest businessman in the world and be a great success, but I think you're doomed to failure because there's always going to be Bill Gates. The moment you redefine your goals to help people in a hopeless cause, you can't fail, because then you're up against insurmountable odds. This was a great lesson my father taught me. I think my father suffered immensely throughout this life because people have always looked on what he's done and said he's bad as opposed to just being ill. I don't think he had friends and I didn't see him for years either. I think he must have been terribly lonely and sad.'

My meeting with Clive left me with a mix of emotions. His passion and enthusiasm for his work is admirable, and, like many people who meet him or hear him speak, I became instantly sympathetic to his cause. In his book *Bad Men*, about Guantanamo, it is clear how important humour is to him, and no doubt his public school education would have prepared him well for some of his experiences. When I recall some of the indignities and humiliations of boarding school life, laughter always seemed to be the best medicine.

Clive is lucky to feel an innate sense of joy in his life, and it is remarkable that he can find that in the world he lives in through his work. It is a challenge many of us would love to respond to in our own lives. His turning point away from the more conventional existence that his upbringing would suggest appeared to be writing an essay on the death penalty, but the reality for him is that it had been more of an evolution influenced by a number of factors, including his relationship with his father. His obvious compassion for his dad, who had struggled with mental illness, was also visible in his relationships with those on death row. I can imagine too that his sense of fairness and anger at any kind of injustice would have developed in his early years.

Altruism is a guiding principle in Clive's life, and his desire to help others is at the heart of his natural joyfulness. His passion for justice has taken him to some of the darkest prisons, yet he has not allowed the injustices that he has witnessed to overshadow the underlying joy he feels – for his family; for humanity; and, most tellingly, for life itself. Perhaps the greatest crime of all occurs when we become too wrapped up in negativity, when we become, according to Clive, 'afraid to live'. Living with courage and optimism is something to which we can all aspire.

4

JOHN WOOD

The moment I heard about John Wood, I was intrigued. Although he is American, his upbringing had certain parallels with mine, and like Clive he had discovered a social need and decided to help. The story of his move from the business world to founding a charity had obvious similarities with my own, although his background as a senior executive at Microsoft had given him a far greater public platform for his work. He had been given a significant amount of responsibility at a fairly young age, as I had, but had later begun to question the life he was leading.

John had a key turning point in his life when he visited a simple village school on a trek in Nepal and realized that he could transform their education by supplying books for a library. Within little more than a year, John took the dramatic and courageous step of leaving Microsoft to found his successful non-profit organization Room to Read, with a mission to transform education for millions of children in undeveloped countries. Since the year 2000, Room to Read has won many prestigious awards, founding more than 7,000 libraries and over 700 schools across nine countries in Asia and Africa.

The similarities with my own story made me keen to know whether he had faced some of the personal challenges that I had when I decided to change my life. From what I read about him, he did not appear to have any regrets about any of the paths he had chosen. By leaving Microsoft, he had made many sacrifices in financial terms and in his private life, but it was apparent he saw those as positive steps, particularly as he now had time for family and friends.

I met him in London on one of his many international trips, persuading people to fund his work and checking on his many projects. In every country, he seemed to have a network of devotees ready to respond, and that was clearly the result of his ability to tell his story in a way that worked for his audience. Perhaps I had expected someone with the slightly geeky look of Bill Gates, but I was pleasantly surprised to find that he was an attractive and friendly man. He appeared to be a fairly typical American corporate type, with his short greying hair, blazer and striped shirt, but his casual R. M. Williams boots gave a hint of his other life, often spent travelling in difficult circumstances. He was softly spoken and intense with a seriousness that contrasted with many of my British interviewees, who often used humour to describe difficult situations. He was clearly a very bright man who preferred to reel off figures rather than to delve too much into his own emotions. Thankfully, he was very articulate as he began to tell me about his upbringing and the corporate life that had led up to his turning point.

'My parents were fairly simple people, if you will, in terms of their upbringing. They both valued education highly, as my father had grown up in a poor family with an alcoholic father and was the only one of seven children to go to university. That was as a result of the GI bill in the US. Education had been his ticket out, and he had ended up as a civil engineer working for Boeing. He had earned his way into the middle class. He always trusted education and told us it was important to get good grades.

'I was the youngest of three children, and most of my childhood was spent in a fairly conservative small town in Pennsylvania. I was probably the most diligent child, the one who listened to my father. I read a lot, went to the library quite often and got good grades. My brother and sister were quite a bit older so I was sort of an only child and books always filled a void for me. My mother was a full-time mum, always there for us – a very good, supportive person. I always wanted to please my parents.

'Both my parents were involved in small-town charity work. My mother volunteered for the Red Cross, and my dad volunteered for the fire department. I remember once when I was eight years old and the river flooded and we all went down to fill sandbags for hours on end to try to block the river. In many ways this is the best kind of volunteering, as it really holds a community together, and this was something I was to see in Nepal. My parents didn't have money to give but they would always give their time.

'Religion was not a big part of life. My mother is Lutheran and my dad Catholic, and he ended up taking us to church to give her a chance to stay in bed on a Sunday. As I got older we still went through the motions of going to church, but it seemed like every year we went less and less frequently to the point that, when I was twelve or thirteen, we probably went on Christmas Eve and Easter and that was it. Even then I didn't really understand it – the same guy was up there doing the same thing time and time again, and I was like, "This is boring; we do this every week."

'I eventually went to the University of Colorado, which is a little college in the Rocky Mountains. I loved to ski when I was a kid, and I wanted to get away from the east coast. My sister had moved to Boulder, Colorado for her job, and that gave me a launching pad. I studied finance and economics, and then went on to do my MBA at Kellogg Business School at Northwestern University in Chicago. Ironically, I remember when I was there a fellow student, who is now a great friend, ran a group called "Business with a heart", and I thought, "Who the h**l wants to do something like that?"

'After graduate school, I did two years in banking, which I did not like at all. It was the most boring, staid environment, and

I thought everyone was like thirty-two going on seventy, and "Oh, what did you do this weekend?" "I washed the car..." – like that's exciting. I was just burning with desire to get out and see the world and do something different. I thought I would use banking as a way to live overseas, but then Microsoft came along and a friend of mine who was working as a recruiter there called me out of the blue and asked me if I'd like to come out to Seattle for an interview as a project manager. That was 1991, and it got me out of banking and out of the Midwest.

'Microsoft was a really exciting environment to work in in the 1990s, because the company was growing so quickly and there were always new challenges. There was no road map for what we were doing, just as there isn't now with Room to Read. There was no operating manual, and you could be given a lot of responsibility at a really young age. I would be told to get on a plane, go to Taipei, figure this problem out; get on a plane, go to South Africa and brief the South African media, and I'm like, "They're really sending me to do all this?" I'm thirty years old and I've no idea what I'm doing and I'm still learning and I was not at all a technology geek.

'It was a really fun and interesting place to be. It had its challenges, as I worked extreme hours, but I didn't mind. I was young, single and trying to prove myself in the world and it was very, very lucrative financially. I remember when Bill Gates got engaged to Melinda, people said, "Oh, thank God they got engaged; that means Bill will slow down and get easier," and I was like, "You know, if you don't want to work hard, don't work here. Go work for somebody else, because some of us do want the company to do well." Every day, we looked at the stock price – we knew where it was going, and we wanted to make the sacrifice.

'In 1995, aged thirty-one, I was offered the job of Marketing Director for the whole Asia-Pacific division including Australia, which meant moving to Sydney. It was a huge responsibility but I loved the travel. I had a 25-person team working for me.

I'd never managed a big team before, but I'd been managed by managers who were masterful at leading teams, so I thought I'd implement everything I'd learned at Microsoft and at graduate school about leadership and management. I think I was good at it; I got rated in the top third of my peer group at Microsoft, and my team loved working for me. It was all so new and I had to run the internet unit out there, which was challenging but fun, as we did extremely well at it and we were like the coolest group within Microsoft Australia.

'However, by the end of 1997, I had decided to leave the company for a while. There were a lot of things I wanted to do in my life that I knew I would never have time for if I was still at Microsoft because it was an all-consuming, all-demanding position, and I thought I could always come back as a consultant. I knew I had to take some time out to figure out what it was that I wanted to do with the rest of my adult life. I also knew that my family and friends had suffered because of my job and just couldn't rely on me. In the end, I ended up travelling for a while but still came back and did a bunch of projects for Microsoft.

'It was during this time that I first went to Nepal, which was the real turning point in my life. It wasn't a kind of epiphany moment – it just wasn't that immediate – but I saw a need and wanted to help. I was trekking with a group of people, and on the way I was invited to see this school by a man called Pasupathi, who was the District Resource person for that part of Nepal, the Lampung Province. I think he had a number of schools in the district, and we were literally just drinking tea and talking to him at this little teahouse and asking him what the school system is like, and he said, "Why don't you come along and see our school tomorrow?"

'I thought, naively, that we were going to entertain the kids and do a guest lecture. We got to the school and it was obvious to me that the conditions that the kids were learning in were just appalling. They had a dirt floor and a leaky roof and they just had benches for the kids to sit on and no desks. They had 450 students in this school, and it looked like it probably should have held half that number. Then they invited us to see the school's library, and that was really the turning point when we walked into this library and it was just this empty room completely devoid of books. I didn't want to be obnoxious, but I asked, "Where exactly are your books?" and he said, "Oh, they're in the cabinet in the back...," and ironically the padlock was on to keep the kids away from them as they had so few and they were precious. When they unlocked the treasure trove of books, they had about twenty, and they were all things that backpackers had left behind. Everything that happened just kind of stemmed from that moment. It sounds so simple, but it was just that one school and I talked to the headmaster and he said, "Perhaps you'll come back some day with books."

'The illiteracy rate is 70 per cent in Nepal, and I guess I put three things together: one is the illiteracy rate is high; two, there are no books; and three, people are only making a dollar a day. If you look at the wealthiest societies in the world and their GNP per person, they all have literacy rates of above 90 per cent, and if you look at the twenty poorest societies in the world, they all have literacy rates below 20 per cent. I didn't really know if I'd necessarily become the "pied piper" of third world libraries, but just that one school and the headmaster's request for me to come back became this interesting thing for the next sixteen days as I was trekking. I knew that I would get back to real life and it would be taking me in the usual frantic directions, but I also knew that I wanted to act. I didn't know that I would, because I think that all of us in our lives can have these things happen, but you soon realize you didn't get around to doing anything about it.

'I think part of the reason I eventually acted was because I sent an email to various friends around the world requesting books, and that ended up putting pressure on me to do something. I thought it would be fun to get friends involved, as I had done before with a project to help the homeless with food at Christmas. I had seen a problem and worked out a solution, just as I was to do with the book project. The result of my email was 3,000 books in the first month.

'By now, I was involved with Microsoft again. I had a new girlfriend who wanted to move to China with her job and I thought I would do some consulting there too, but the guy who ran Microsoft China wanted me as his right-hand man running business development. I got to Beijing to start my job in January of 1999 and returned to Nepal with the books that spring. My father came with me and it was just incredible to personally deliver the books, going along the same path I'd been walking a year earlier. This time there were 3,000 books, bundled on the backs of donkeys, and we were going to visit all these different schools. It was amazing to watch the reaction of the communities, with literally hundreds of people turning out to welcome us and open up their homes to us. The teachers invited us for dinner, people played music, and children picked flowers in the forest to give us.

'It seemed like we'd done so little – I mean, all we'd done was to collect a bunch of used books with one email and paid $800 to ship them all over to Nepal – yet there was such an outpouring of thanks. It felt incredible; it felt absolutely amazing. In the photos, I had the biggest, goofiest grin on my face the whole day. It wasn't comparable with anything in my working life because it wasn't about making rich people richer; it was doing something unique for the kids. In certain ways it felt sort of karmic because I had grown up with books, and books made me who I am and gave me a good education, which got me to Microsoft and the millions of dollars of stock options. I really felt like I was just paying back a bit of my good fortune to the world.

'This, of course, turned out to be one of the most difficult times for me in the end. I was feeling so good about being there with my father in that community, but the next day I had to head back to my real life with Microsoft in Beijing. I thought to myself, "I think I've made a colossal error: I think it was wrong to move to Beijing; I think it was wrong to go back to Microsoft. I think *this* is what I want to do with my life – this feels so much better." I had negotiated this time out with my boss as a one-off, but once I was back, I would have to be completely focused on a very demanding job. I just wasn't ready for this to end.

'When I got back I spent a lot of time soul-searching, and I wrote my journals for hours and hours. I really struggled with my decision because it was going to be a complete break with what I knew, and obviously if you quit twice, you don't get invited to come back a third time. It took me six to eight weeks to come to grips with it, but one incident helped focus me.

'I was back in Seattle on a business trip in 1999 when the United States had bombed the Chinese Embassy in Belgrade during the Yugoslav war. Nobody at Microsoft was looking out for us expats; they didn't really seem to care. My girlfriend was in Beijing, and I had to try to get her out because there were anti-American riots in the embassy district, where we lived. Expats were being told to get out of China, and yet Microsoft was doing nothing to be the least bit supportive. At one point, I called the emergency expat hotline for two consecutive days of the weekend. Nobody picked up and the voicemail box was full, and when somebody from HR finally called me back on Monday, the first thing she said was, "Wow, you're staying in an expensive hotel – who's paying for that?" I realized at that point that the company isn't going to look out for me, and I had been so hesitant to quit because I felt like I'd made this vow to go back to the company and make good on this promise to help them expand in China, but at that point in time I thought, "You know what, they're not looking out for me..." so in a certain sense it was a blessing because it made it easier for me to cut the ties.

'After this, I went back to tell my girlfriend and then my boss. I think "anger" is the best way to sum up the reaction. My boss felt really let down, as he had been warned not to hire me as I had quit before. I told him, "I have to follow my heart right now. My heart is just not into China; it's not into this job." I don't think he understood and I don't know that I articulated it all that well as I was struggling with a lot of things at that point, so it could be that the fault was partly mine. I felt it was my deal and I needed to work it through myself.

'When I look back now at my own journey, I couldn't have scripted it better. I learned so much in my eight years at Microsoft, and I think I got out at the exact right time. It's good for me now, because people do take me much more seriously as a successful entrepreneur, and you can get a meeting with the CEO of a company more easily than others can. I don't regret anything; I just feel lucky. I don't know if it was fate or if it was destiny or if it was just incredible serendipity.

'It did take me a bit of time to get over leaving Microsoft. My identity was so wrapped up in it, and it was about a year before I stopped telling people I used to be at Microsoft and started just talking about Room to Read. It was partly a status thing. The hard part was the fact that I thought all the people I respected would be supportive, but it wasn't the case. In some ways, you find your true friends, and I have met so many great people since doing this.

'I founded Room to Read on business principles but kept it all very small at first, running it on a shoestring budget. I could work for free while I started to raise the money, although in retrospect I would have hired more people more quickly if I knew then what I know now, and I would have asked funders to pay for some overhead. In the first year, I wanted to build a donor base and a team out in Nepal and after that to start scouting out other countries. I had said my aim was to help 10 million children from day one. I was told it was hubristic to go for 10 million, and I said, "You know what, if we're not going to go big on this, there's no reason to do it – let's go back to the profit world and make millions more and just donate that to other organizations…" I always wanted to be as focused on results as we had been at Microsoft.

'In the beginning I had wondered whether that would have been the right move, but since we began I've raised $85 million. There's just no way I would have earned that at Microsoft, so in a certain sense it's better because I'm using my kind of leadership skills and salesmanship skills to get a lot of capital that might have otherwise gone to the symphony or the opera or groups that don't need it so much and have instead put it into the communities in Cambodia and Vietnam that need it more. There is a deservedly negative view of America in the developing world, which has worsened significantly in the last few years. This is a way to change that.

'There is a bit of spirituality in my life. I am very agnostic, against organized religion, but I definitely believe in a God and I pray to that God. I pay attention to spiritual things in the world, but other than Buddhism – which I believe is as much a philosophy as it is a religion – I've never really found a religion that I like. I like to borrow elements, and I've come up with my own unique blend of religion and philosophy. I don't think I will ever be an absolutely good person, but I just feel like an imperfect guy doing what I can.

'My philosophy is very simple. If you end up getting a lot given to you in life, that doesn't make you a good person. The question is what do you do with that good fortune. There are a lot of people out there who make a lot and have a lot but they're not happy, and I know a lot of people who make a lot and have a lot and they do a lot for others, and they're the ones who are absolutely truly happy. I think the closest it comes in religious terms is the teachings of the Dalai Lama and the art of happiness, which says that if you're giving some of your good fortune away and sharing it with others, it actually accrues back to you many, many times over. There's no value equation – it's all spiritual; it's all karmic; it's all about feeling good about doing what you do, and in my case it's interesting that so many people in the world really treat me well because of who I am and what I do.

'There is a certain part of me that feels like I'm living this prolonged adolescence because I'm single and I've no kids and I'm still renting and I don't own a home or any of that stuff, but then a part of me feels like I am being hard on myself, as I have taken on responsibility for the education of well over a million kids to date and 10 million by a certain point in time. I've definitely upped the ante for a lot of people I know, who look at me and they say, "Wow, you're giving your life for this? The least I can do is write a cheque, or the least I can do is endow a school or throw you a cocktail party and tell all my friends to donate to you." A huge number of my old friends and a huge number of my new friends have become more involved in philanthropy as a result of that influence, and it has given them some optimism that America can do something good.

'There is a lot of dark stuff in the world, but I feel that all you can do is shine a light in the darkness and help to make it a lot more light. It is hard to think about an epitaph, but I guess I would want it to say that I was "a fairly average, imperfect human being who did what he could while he was on this earth to give kids the chance to learn...".

'In terms of philanthropy, I tell people if you go into business make sure that you have philanthropy in your life. I always say don't do this as a minor choice. Going into the business world is a good thing even for a would-be social entrepreneur, but push your company to be a responsible, corporate citizen; push your friends and your co-workers to work with you on some outside project – mentor kids or fund schools or clean water projects in the Third World. When I talk at MBA schools, I am amazed at the crowds that turn up and how engaged they are.'

Many of the points John made about his own journey and his success would inspire anyone thinking of changing their own life. His turning point was the result of seeing the hardship of others rather than of any tragedy in his own life, and like me he had the significant advantage of a financial cushion to allow him to take the next steps. I am all too aware that this is not the case for most people. However, John has had the courage to put the advantages he has had of a good education and stellar career at Microsoft to the best possible use, something that we can all learn from, regardless of our circumstances.

As John spoke, there were constant reminders of my own early life. He reminded me of the value of an upbringing in which education is really prized and the advantage of having parents who always looked out for their own community. Like John, I had really enjoyed the challenges and responsibilities of my early career and found the departure from my business harder than I had expected. Perhaps more poignantly, his visit to the school in Nepal seemed to be a direct parallel to my visit to a school in Easterhouse, a tough part of Glasgow. I was also profoundly shocked by the bleak surroundings that children were expected to learn in and left feeling deeply moved, unsure of what I could possibly do about it. It is easy to assume these kinds of situations only happen in underdeveloped countries.

John's simple philosophy – that it is what you do with your good fortune that counts and that happiness comes from doing things for others – is a challenge for any of us. It is not always about money or even having a great deal of spare time, although many people gain so much from volunteering in their community. It can even be as simple as remembering to smile or to have a chat with the person who serves us in the supermarket. Britain has a remarkable history of charity work, but those who work in that area don't always get the respect they deserve. Perhaps in time more people will have the courage to make the choice that John has made and see success not in terms of personal gain, but of the positive difference we can make to others and the world around us.

5

FRANNY McGRATH

I have always appreciated the upbringing I had. Even when I found family life challenging, I knew that I was loved. My parents and many of my teachers taught me a set of values, such as honesty and integrity, that have been key to my life. As my life changed and I met young people from troubled backgrounds, I realized just how lucky I had been. It was hard for me to imagine or even understand the difficult circumstances in which many young Scots had grown up through no fault of their own. I recall my first trip to Easterhouse and being shown a flat where a boy of fourteen had died of a heroin overdose – the youngest boy in Scotland to die that way. It was suspected that it had been given to him by his mother's boyfriend. When the police arrived, the flat was very empty and stark – even the doorframes and the skirting had been removed. The only thing left apart from the boy lying dead in the corner was a tank full of exotic fish and a large TV set. I simply could not take in the reality of a world like that.

I had heard of Franny through my work at ProjectScotland and had met some of the young people whose lives had been changed by their involvement with the YMCA in Perth where he worked. I gathered that Franny played a key role in their lives and was curious to meet him. When I first saw him, I was surprised by how young he seemed. In his trendy cords, V-neck jumper, white T-shirt, cool specs and short blond hair, he looked almost like a young designer from an advertising agency. I was amazed to find out that he had a teenage son and two daughters and that he was in his late thirties. I put this down to a combination of good Scottish air (he lives in the lovely Highland town of Aberfeldy) and perhaps his religious faith. It came as an even bigger surprise to discover that his previous life had been very different and had involved time in prison.

I had asked him why he thought he made such a good role model and mentor for some of the troubled and damaged young people he was helping, and after a brief pause, he told me that it was because he had been there himself. He spoke briefly, and in a matter-of-fact way, without bitterness, about his past life, which had been destroyed by heroin and by many years in prison, particularly in Scotland's toughest jail, Barlinnie. He mentioned his redemption through his faith and the love of his wife as the turning points that changed his life. He was happy to tell his story, as he often does to the young people around him. I admired his bravery and honesty, as I know he is concerned about the impact telling it can have on his family.

'I grew up on a housing scheme in Saltcoats, on the west side of Scotland, near Glasgow. I was the youngest in the family and my parents had separated, but from an early age I think things didn't seem to fit for me; I just didn't fit in, probably for a variety of reasons. My two older sisters, Angela and Mary, had already been sent to the local Catholic school before my stepfather came on the scene. My mother obviously wanted to keep us all together at the same school but my stepfather was quite a bigoted Protestant. He had been brought up by his father, who was a bit of a maniac and was involved in the Orange Walks [involving members of the Protestant Orange Order] and the Masons. Catholics stayed up the stairs from them and they hated them for it. He influenced me a lot, so from an early age I supported Rangers [the traditionally Protestant football team] and was involved in going to see the Orange Walks passing in the town. But for me to then be sent to a Catholic school meant it was kind of a double life, because I was in the primary school and everybody else there was quite avid Celtic [the traditionally Catholic team] supporters and brought up in the tradition of the Catholic faith, whereas when I go back home it's kind of, "Oh, don't listen to that; it's a load of s**t..." or worse language.

'I didn't feel I fitted in at all at the school, and soon got into a lot of trouble. I got involved in gambling at an early age at primary school because I'd be betting people for Rangers to win on Saturday, especially if it was against Celtic, and before I knew it, by the time I was going into primary six and seven (aged ten or so), I was already down the street shoplifting. I was fighting every now and again, and I'd get into trouble for things like that and shoplifting at the weekends, and obviously that starts to progress. By the time I got into secondary school, I was starting to take tablets such as Valium, and the shoplifting was starting to escalate to stealing bottles of vodka or whisky or steaks with my wee gang. We'd go and sell them to all our neighbours, ending up with forty or fifty quid, which I would then take to the amusement arcades.

'It gave me some security to be part of a gang and we knew each other quite well, although we were always fighting for position to a certain extent. I remember once they all chased me home and started writing something mean on my front door. My stepfather actually sent me back outside with a pick-shaft and I smashed one of them over the head with it – a great example of my stepfather's influence.

'It is really hard to expect a child to do well when most weekends my mum and stepfather would be drunk. They would go to the pub, bring their friends back and there would be bit of a party in the house, and maybe I'm exaggerating a bit but I often remember waking up in the morning and my mum would have a black eye and my stepfather's head would be cut because my mum had hit him over the head with a bottle and the living room would be smashed up. You would hear that as a child at night as well – the fighting and the screaming – and you'd be in your room pretty scared and thinking, "Here we go again," and obviously you kind of got used to that and it almost became normality.

'As for my time at school, in general I was not interested. I remember I had one teacher who stood out, my maths teacher. I didn't get on with him and I was a pain in the arse but I remember actually doing a bit of work one day, and him putting on it, "Worked extremely hard today, well done...," and I was quite happy – well, it was a bit of praise from somebody. I remember him saying, "Praise where praise is due," and it did mean something to me. I held on to that and thought it's quite nice to get recognized for doing something. Otherwise, I enjoyed sport. I don't think I was particularly thick, but I just didn't enjoy learning in that environment and would look for any excuse to put other people off their work and get into a bit of trouble. I got suspended a couple of times, and basically I left at the earliest opportunity when I was fifteen and went straight onto a Youth Training Scheme. By the time I was sixteen, I suppose I had been done for a number of shopliftings, breach of the peace and I think I'd been done for a house break-in too and for loads of assaults. I didn't like getting caught by the police, but apart from a couple of slaps, my parents didn't do much. I soon got sacked from the YTS but I was still interested in football, going to all the Rangers games trying to find a buzz. I soon joined the Rangers gang and would go off to other cities looking for a fight with rival gangs.

'Obviously it's the whole influence of growing up that affects how you behave outside as well. One of the happy things I remember growing up was camping with my friends, but one night I was in the tent out the back door with my friend, aged about fourteen, and we heard a big commotion going on, at about midnight. I ran round and I saw my mum getting carried into the ambulance, and I went into the living room and my stepfather's sitting there with his head in his hands and the table's all smashed up and there's tablets lying about because my mum was on sleeping tablets by that time. He's sitting there and saying to me, "… Just hit me, hit me, I'm this, I'm that…" and stuff like that, so obviously they must have had a bit of a fight and were drinking too much and she tried taking an overdose on the tablets and an ambulance got called.

'Around then, she had three strokes in total over different periods of time and lost the use of all the left side of her body, including her arm and her leg, probably because of the alcohol abuse over many years and all the smoking and everything else and probably the stress of trying to bring up the three of us. I remember going up to see her in hospital and I could hardly look at her. I found it very difficult to show any emotion at that age, and to the best of my recollection, there wasn't much love shown within the family. I felt like crying, I felt like giving her a cuddle, but you just didn't know how to handle that.

'Not long after I was sacked from the YTS, I began to realize that I was soon going to end up in prison, so I decided to go and stay with my sister who lived in London. I found out my real dad was there now. I hadn't wanted to see him much before but I found the stories of the trouble he got in quite exciting. I went over to his house in Acton, and the first thing he did was to throw me a big lump of hash and say, "Eat that son, get that down ye'…"; that was my introduction to him. I was obviously stoned out of my face for about two days. What happened down there was that they were scamming all sorts of things and exploiting the benefits system. Before long, I was involved, but I ended up getting caught and returned to Scotland. I got given my first prison sentence, which was for nine months. I remember my first walk into Barlinnie, the adult prison with guys in for whatever, murderers, bank robbers and all the rest of it. At that time it was very chaotic, with the prisoners virtually running the place, and I was quite scared. I was a young boy and at the same time I was trying to put on this kind of bravado as if you don't care. I was terrified inside, and after you go through the reception, you get put into this wee box and you're left there for hours and then you get shown up into the hall and you're climbing up the stairs going towards your prison cell with all these big men walking about. I remember getting put in my cell and the door slamming, and the place was absolutely disgusting. I sat down on the bed and was probably just about to burst into tears or something but luckily two older guys appeared, saying, "How's it going, wee man?" They knew me from Saltcoats, which seemed to make everything better.

'Eventually I was moved to the young offenders' prison at Polmont, which was better and less terrifying. It was still "slopping out" [a bucket as a toilet] in the cells, but we had to keep them all looking perfect. Every Saturday there would be a governor's inspection, and you had to get your bed made and everything folded and I had a wee jigsaw at the front of my door saying "welcome" to make it homely, but the guy just opened the door and kicked it up the cell because you weren't allowed anything on the floor. I'd get visits now and then from my mum and stepfather but not my friends. My dad came to visit and would manage to bring me some hash or Valium although we'd get strip-searched now and again. I didn't enjoy the experience of prison life, but it didn't make enough of an impression to stop me coming back either.'

Franny admitted that it wasn't long before he headed back to London and started dealing in drugs and other scams for his brother-in-law and dad. He doesn't remember feeling any guilt because it just seemed normal in that environment. He was soon getting to know a variety of prisons in the south, like Rochester and Felton, none of which provided any real opportunities for his rehabilitation. He also met a girl, Mags, and at the age of twenty fathered his first son, Stephen, which led him back to Scotland to try to find a more stable life for them all. They lived on benefits as he admits to not really knowing how to get a job.

Before long he was back to dealing in drugs and stealing. After one particularly drunken night out, he got involved in a fight and ended up slashing a man's face with a bottle, leading to a four-year prison sentence and a return to Barlinnie. By this time he had married his girlfriend, and by asking her to bring him drugs in prison, landed her in prison for a couple of months. During their brief time together, she became pregnant with his second child, Kayleigh. It was clear that Franny was repeating the same cycle he had grown up with and his children would be the next generation to suffer the consequences.

'I was totally irresponsible. I cared about my kids in that kind of way you say, "Yes, I love my kids and this and that…," and I probably did, but I didn't show it with the way I was living. I didn't take any responsibility; I lived a reckless life and that seemed acceptable, that was almost normality for us. By the time I got out in July 1994, my wife had had another child to this other guy and I'd started to see somebody else who came and visited me while I was in prison. Mags asked me to take the two kids while she went into hospital for a minor operation. I got a phone call that night to say that she had died. The surgery had gone wrong, but she was put on the recovery ward and died from internal bleeding. I had to go and see her body as I was still legally her husband, and the next day I had to break the news to the kids (then five and three) that they wouldn't be seeing their mum again. It's one of the hardest things I've ever done – it's unbearable – and by this time I was a heroin addict because I'd been dabbling in heroin in prison and continued to take it when I got out. I even got my dad addicted to heroin when he ended up in Barlinnie too. What happened was bad but it didn't stop me taking drugs. I got out of prison for a bit and had a house up in Airdrie [near Glasgow] – me and this girl Maria and her wee boy and my two kids – but I would just go out and leave her to it and then I'd be back in jail again for this and that.

'I suppose, at different times in prison, going through the whole thing, I'd think, "This is the last time, I'm no' doing this again." Then you'd get back outside; you'd get involved in the same influences, the same different things, nothing really there, nothing prepared for you going out, so before you know it, you're caught up in everything that's happening again. In prison I kind of got along with folk, but mainly I kept to myself as long as I was getting my drugs. I was selling them, getting people to throw bucket-loads over the wall. By now I was going to the worksheds and working on sewing machines and I did a further education course. I read a lot of stuff and for some reason was always trying to disprove Christianity. My sister and brother-in-law were Christians now and living a decent life. They would write to me and send books to try to get me to change my life, but instead I would spend time trying to disprove that Christianity could possibly be real.

'I had been at a Catholic school and I remember doing confessions on a Friday. I used to go to the wee box and say, "Aw, I've been stealing, I've been fighting," and it would be, "Go and say twenty Hail Marys and away you go," so I would steal the collection on the way out. I'd done my confirmation as a young lad but none of it meant anything. I remember once hearing the Reverend R. T. Kendall speak in a church in Westminster when I was in London and there was something different: the people seemed happy and it was colourful. He was speaking about Jesus being born again, and my heart started beating and there was a fear in me as well which made me head straight out the door. I even went to see [the evangelist] Billy Graham once when he was preaching at Parkhead, but I was full of Buckfast [a strong tonic wine] and acid so it didn't really make that much sense. But I was starting to think about different things now, that there may be more to life than this. I was ready for a turning point in my life.

'The opportunity came up for me to do this course led by an organization called Unity Enterprise. This was the first time

I'd taken part in something like that, but one of my pals said it was quite good. They had some money to do work with criminals to break the habit of offending by things like training and workshops. I went for an interview with one of the prison officers and Jill, my future wife, was there. The officer said I was a "great guy, no hassle with him", because I was quite quiet and they hadn't a clue about all the stuff I was involved in until later when some of it started to come out. We did this travel stuff as one of the training programmes and you would start to find out, "Oh, there's a whole other world out there and look at all these destinations." You know people go on holiday and people live normal lives and it all sounds quite basic, but for me it was starting to open up a wee bit of a new world.

'I struck up a really good friendship with Jill as well and found we'd actually quite a lot in common although she'd come from a stable background. We both were interested in the meaning of life and discussed Christianity. I wanted nothing more than to accept it; it was kind of, "Well, I'll believe this if God hits me with a bolt of lightning and knocks me on my backside...," but I can't just believe it in my head, you know, I can't just accept it; it's got to be in the heart, it can't be a mind thing. I used to do my best to try to impress her and do well with my work, and I actually got the officers to get me to go down early so I would be there for her coming. But I was still using heroin, still getting people to bring in drugs, and some days I'd go down and I'd be out of my face and it's no' a pretty sight when you see somebody like that, and she'd end up in tears. Meeting Jill was definitely the turning point for me as she was such a big influence at that time. She helped me see that although I had been dealt these cards in life, I now had the choice to say I don't need to continue as I am. She showed me that my skills could be used in a different way and gave me a bit of self-belief. She didn't give up on me when I got into trouble. I went on a drugs course which helped me too.

'When I got out of prison the next time, I was still involved with heroin but I knew I loved Jill and wanted that to work out. I lived with my mother and stepfather; they had much better lives since my mum's stroke, and she had even become a Christian and they were looking after my kids. I got a job at a call centre and Jill would come and visit at weekends. She encouraged me to look for volunteering opportunities and I ended up having a great nine months working with Galloway training, and then the opportunity came up to be a volunteer assistant with the Prince's Trust. During that time, a friend I knew from prison invited me on an Alpha course and I went there, and rather than get this big bolt of lightning out of the sky, I just accepted on one of those nights that Jesus must have been who he said he was and that this is all real for me. It just connected and it was like a light bulb going on in my head. I understood that I didn't have to be perfect for God to accept me. After that, things just seemed to work for me and I even got an invite to meet the Queen. Jill became a Christian three days after me, and we ended up getting married on 28 December 1999, and she was soon pregnant with my youngest daughter, Rebecca. I had begun to think about getting involved in ministry work, and eventually I got the job working with young people here with the YMCA and we moved to Aberfeldy.

'It's been over twelve years since I've been out of trouble and out of prison, and probably ten since I've smoked hash or anything like that. I still have occasional issues with anger after all the years of violence that I witnessed and was involved with but I just have to keep working on that. I know that all the experiences I had have helped me with the work I do here. I always try to make the point to people that you don't need to have been through that to be able to empathize, but I think for me it's a big strength; it's a big advantage. I can work with the young ones from schools; I can work with the young guys that are in and out of prison, that have taken drugs, and I can really understand where they're at.

'I think the biggest thing for me is the faith in my life just now, and I always think I'd like my epitaph to simply say I was a "man of God", somebody who had a real love of God and was therefore able to love the young people that we work with. I would like to be known more for the faith that I had in God and how I lived that out in life rather than anything else. The YMCA has been a massive influence over the past seven years, and I have taken the opportunity – if young people are interested – to share my story, to tell them, "Here's why I believe what I believe, here's what helped me change my life." I'm trying to develop a lot of young people, even within the church as well. I've got six of them that I'm really trying to help develop as young leaders within their faith, learning how to live out their faith within their own environment and the pressures that are involved in that.

'When I look at the lives of many young people, if you strip it all away to the bottom line, you can say family, you can say community, you can say all kinds of different things are important, but the bottom line is that God is missing from people's lives, missing from their families, from the community and from the whole world sometimes. It's not that he's missing, it's just that we don't live within God's plan and purpose for our life and therefore it affects everything. I remember being asked here at my interview, "What are the three biggest things that are affecting young people today?" I said God's the most important one, and then I would say the family, and then I would say the community.'

It is only as I drive home that some of what Franny has told me really begins to sink in – the horrors of his childhood, the all-too-easy and predictable slide into drug addiction and a criminal life. I find myself painfully aware of how few people did anything to help – how easily he was let down by the system and by people who should have been looking out for him. He had no positive role models or mentors in his life, and the prison environment had only made things worse. When I visited the young offenders' prison at Polmont, I was struck by the few opportunities for rehabilitation that existed in this very dehumanizing environment, often as a result of cuts in the budget and overcrowding. In spite of this, I gathered that some boys preferred to be locked up than to be abused at home. The mention of Franny's momentary appreciation by the maths teacher makes me feel a mix of anger and immense sadness. Yet he tells his story without the slightest hint of bitterness, accepting responsibility for his past but using it to help others, to be there for people like him.

It seems strange to think that religious bigotry was almost the starting point for his troubles, and yet it is religion that has been his saviour. I find the simplicity of the way he tells the story, his humility and recognition of his weaknesses almost Christ-like, perhaps even like St Paul himself, who had the first road to Damascus moment.

Franny's turning point was meeting Jill in the prison and finding his faith. Clearly he had been thinking about another way to live but he had never been able to make the real change before. Jill's role was so important – somehow managing to make him feel loved but also refusing to accept his bad behaviour. She reminded him that he had a choice, just as we all do, not to be a victim of his circumstances. Franny may have had two very different lives but it is hard to imagine one without the other.

Once he had managed to escape his past, it was obvious to him that he should start to help others, and his work with the YMCA is the key to that. He is prepared to reach out to young people whom so many would turn away from, and in some ways to put himself at risk. Paula Lowther is one of those young people who has been lucky enough to have him as a mentor and friend. I was keen to talk to her about her life, knowing that she had also had a chaotic upbringing before I met her as a young volunteer at ProjectScotland.

6

PAULA LOWTHER

Paula Lowther is one of the young stars of ProjectScotland, the volunteering charity born out of my own turning point. And her own 'second chance', as she calls it, has enabled her to transform a life of disadvantage and adversity into something meaningful and precious. Franny McGrath was the key to her new life through his work at the Perth YMCA, always looking out for her as her boss, mentor and friend. He told me that ProjectScotland had been the turning point in her life, even giving her the confidence to appear in the charity's advertising campaign and present her story at events all over Scotland. I was keen to understand how that had happened and how her journey differed from those of the many more privileged people I had spoken to.

I drove up to meet her at the YMCA. Perth is a place that does a good job of hiding its problems from public view. It has a smart city centre, and its location on the scenic River Tay makes it a desirable place to live for many. But the city has considerable pockets of disadvantage, too. And the YMCA, while situated in a former church not far from one of the city's beautiful parks, gives you a hint of Perth's less appealing side. Its main room, full of rather tatty sofas, ancient curtains screening off different areas and rather incongruous stone war memorials set into the walls, could be described as quite depressing, until Paula showed me around. Seeing the place through her eyes made me look at it differently, and enabled me to appreciate it as a place of warmth and hope for many people. I also learned that it was soon to be redecorated, thanks to Paula's skills at charming sponsors.

She was much smaller than I had expected from her photographs, and prettier, wearing the typical teenage uniform of jeans and striped T-shirt, with long light brown hair falling over her face. It was hard to tell how old she was, as she clearly possessed a maturity beyond her years. She was a forceful and energetic speaker, and her youth and enthusiasm gave her words a unique quality. At times as she spoke, I couldn't help thinking of the contrast between her life and that of my fourteen-year-old daughter, two years older than Paula had been when she became a young carer for her mother.

I expected a justifiable amount of self-pity from Paula as she discussed her early years. But as I'd discovered with Franny, people who have known hardship often present it in an understated and matter-of-fact way, and in a sense, this made it more shocking. She grew up in Fairfield, an area of Perth that appears in the bottom 15 per cent of the deprivation index in Scotland – and in terms of quality-of-life issues, from drug abuse and ill health to lack of employment and poor educational attainment, that means one thing: there are no easy ways out.

'I'm eighteen and I've lived all my life with both my parents in Fairfield, one of the roughest parts of Perth. I have three brothers – two younger brothers (Joshua, ten and Dylan, eleven), one older (Gareth, twenty-one). It was quite difficult being brought up there, not wearing the best of clothes and all that sort of stuff; it wasn't the best area to be brought up in. My dad used to be a farmer once, probably before I was born, but now he has to look after my mum. She's got a mental illness, and because of that I became a young carer too. She had been in the first stages of her illness, just losing a lot of memory, basically not paying any attention to her kids, when her baby son Jordan died of meningitis when he was about thirty days old. It pushed her right over and she sort of lost it from there.

'The way mum explains it, she hears voices telling her to do bad things, so the first thing that showed from the illness was the self harm. She was doing it secretly but then my dad was noticing it, I was noticing it. My big brother didn't like it at all; he was very angry about it. She was cutting herself and trying to take overdoses. And that was sort of my job from the age of twelve until I left home: I had to hide her medication and give it to her at certain times. So I couldn't go out with my friends a lot 'cause I had to give her her medication.

'Then she was in a mental hospital, the Murray Royal, for a year, and that was over Christmas too. That was the worst year of my life 'cause I had so much to do... I was about fourteen or fifteen, and I had to make sure my brothers got to school, clean the house, go shopping. I had to do all these things, and going to school was just a nightmare... I hated it.

'My dad was there... but he used to like to drink quite a lot. He was quite a heavy drinker back then and my mum had this illness. I don't know what was worse, but I wouldn't say he was an alcoholic. But he did enjoy a drink and when he did get drunk, I'd sort of have to look after things in the house and that, go shopping and make sure my brothers were OK and in bed. Because I was the girl, I was having to do the dishes and having to do more of the housework while my brothers were on the computer. I hated school 'cause I had so much on my mind about what I had to do when I got home and did I take the washing out or stuff like that. So I just didn't like school at all.

'The first year had been all right... I guess I started mucking around with the wrong sort of people, especially the boys. I saw them shouting at the teachers, throwing stones at windows, and I thought, "Well I could do that too," you know; it looked all right. I tried smoking hash and I tried drinking alcohol 'cause I've seen it all in my family, and I got in trouble a lot for different things like that at school. I basically left in second year 'cause I skived for like two years. I've been excluded so many times it was unbelievable. I broke my teacher's nose. I was truanting from school, and me and my friends were runnin' and went through a swing door and I swung it back and it hit my teacher. After that, I just lost care for anything 'cause my mum was in hospital for that full year. I just done everything wrong, although I enjoyed it at the time 'cause I thought it was all right, but I broke into everywhere, and I just had a laugh with my friends. I became so cheeky that the teachers wouldn't say anything to me 'cause they'd know I'd just answer back.

'One good thing that did happen at school was that I had a really good guidance teacher, Miss Angus. She got me a Young Carers Award when I was fifteen and I was in Dundee with mum. She was really proud when I got given a big shield and I got £200 for a charity. It was like the first proper achievement, and after that I really wanted to get back into school, but I found it really hard 'cause I felt that the teachers thought, "She's just the same person; she's going to come into my classroom and interrupt me." I wanted to go back into science, but I had really tortured the teacher in that class, so I just had to sit outside at a desk, or sit in the head teacher's office with a desk, which I didn't like much. I wanted to try and do my Standard Grades, but I was thinking too much, "I'm gonna fail. I'm gonna fail and I'm never gonna get anywhere." Basically I didn't turn up for any of my exams anyway, so I left with nothing but an Access Maths. I went to college for a year, just to get away from school, but the only things you get from there are childcare and hairdressing, and I tried childcare 'cause hairdressing's not my kind of thing. I enjoyed college, learning brand new things, but I failed my tests there, because I was still with my old friends from school and wasn't paying attention.

'I think because I saw my mum and dad not working, and they still seemed to have enough money – dad got financial support for being a carer – I thought I would be OK. It seemed normal, even though my mum was unwell and dad was having to look after her. It was hard for him. He's just a normal guy and he would like to go out and work, but my mum's not allowed to go out and have a cleaning job, she's not allowed to drive, she's not allowed to cook, she's not allowed to have my little brothers on her own, she's not allowed, basically, to do anything. She's not allowed to go to local clubs. There was a daytime club she used to go to that involved a lot of people like her, just sitting in a room and talking, but they banned her from it, saying she was a danger to society and the people there, because she was unwell one day and shouted and lost it a bit.

'I was angry about that and I went down there and asked how she could be a danger when she spends time with my little brother and does lots of things. I won my carer award for being seen as a person, not a label, and I say that to everyone when I talk about my mum. It's important that people don't have just one image about mental illness.

'It was very tough when my mum was away in hospital for a year. I used to go up and see her all the time – each night I'd run up and see her. I suppose it was just living in a house full of boys – I missed my mum a lot that year. We've always been close, we still are nowadays, like inseparable you know; we do a lot of things together. The house would just be normal, but there'd be no mum around for my little brothers; I always found that kinda hard. I felt like I was under a lot of pressure, but I couldn't be independent for myself; I had to be independent for everyone else. The year did pass quite quick, but she was in over Christmas, and that hit me 'cause Christmas was always a big thing in my house. She got out afterwards and she was a bit better for a while, but then she lost it again, and it just goes on and on.

'Now I am living away from my mum and it was hard at first. At one point, she was getting worse and worse and I had to run home one day 'cause she was crying on the phone. I just couldn't take it any more after what I saw, and I was starting to think I was getting the illness too. I'm not moving on from my parents, but from living in a house where three brothers share a room and my baby brother died.

'I can't really remember much about his death and there aren't any pictures around, 'cause my mum finds it really hard to have any of them in the house. But I do think of him with my two little brothers either side of him, and that makes me want to look after them more. I feel a lot for them: if they're getting bullied at school or being bullied in the area, I've a lot to say. I go out there and try and sort a lot of it out, 'cause my mum's not able to. I just think of him in a good way, you know. I had a dream of him, that the ambulance went up into the sky with a big light, and 'cause I am a Christian now, I think of him more as up there, instead of just lost somewhere, which really helps.

'I started hearing about Christianity when I began to go to the Saturday night youth club at the YMCA when I was about thirteen, even though sometimes it was rubbish and we would be glued [high on glue]. Me and my two friends thought it was fun to go down and take the mickey out of the Christians. As we got to be the oldest in the group, we were asked to take on more responsibility and lead things. We used to think we were quite hard and we thought, "Naw, we're not leadin' it," and they said, "We don't want to throw you out; we'd rather you come in and do stuff with us," but we were like, "Naw." So we used to sit outside the YMCA and cause trouble – drink and throw bottles and things and just wind them all up. I seemed to be the only one that came into the YMCA again, out of all my friends, and eventually started taking more responsibility.

'That's when I met Franny, 'cause the Big Red Bus [a mobile youth café] was getting decorated and he needed help. Me and my friends were stoned when they asked us, but the next week, we decorated the bus, and we won an award for it. Franny is a good guy, he was a Christian, but we still accepted him as a cool guy. After he did the Bus project he left to go to the Prince's Trust and encouraged me to do the twelve-week team programme course. We had to do a team challenge, and I wanted to do something to help young carers like me. We raised the money to take forty young carers out tenpin bowling in Dundee and gave them gifts and stuff 'cause it was near Christmas. 'Cause I'm a young carer, I stood up and spoke to the group and they loved it, and I saw then that I can change people.

'They were all smiling that night and my Young Carers teacher was like, "Well done Paula; you've done so well," and my whole team loved it. It was just a good experience, one that did change me, but not in the way that I was motivated, or ready, to go and do more at that stage. Then at the end of the programme I had my first chance, standing up in public, doing my final presentation up on stage, in front of 130 people, with the Oscar Awards theme. I was up first and I basically hogged the stage – I loved it that much being up there – and everyone else was like, "Paula, it's us now," and I was like, "Naw, naw, I'm just gonna keep talking." I was on such a buzz afterwards. I was like, "I can do this now."

'I had enjoyed the programme but I just didn't want a job. I'd never been to an interview, I hated the thought of them; they scared me that much, it's unbelievable. I can do one now but at that point I thought, "I'm not going in for an interview." So doing Get Ready for Work at the YMCA was my easiest option, but I ended up getting dismissed from that.

'My friend had broken her arm and had sort of painkillers, and we had come in that day with a hangover so we tried taking some tablets, but we ended up going crazy 'cause the pills weren't what they should have been. We were sick and fainting all over the place, and I was given a written warning by the leader and I told him to shove it and said the F-word thirty-seven times – the whole building heard me. I had one of the biggest temper rages I ever had. I flung a chair and finally got removed from the building. It wasn't a good thing for me when I was drinking as it always made me more emotional and angry. After that I ended up sitting in the house for ages just doing nothing.

'I was scared to go back into the YMCA 'cause I know I done something wrong, but Franny phoned me and said there's a new thing called ProjectScotland and I should come in and hear about it. I was nervous to go in so I didn't turn up the first time, but he phoned me again and I did go in and this was the turning point for me in my life. If it wasn't for ProjectScotland, I don't know what would have happened. It's massive for me 'cause to me it's changed everything, like my whole life.

'I was told that I could start on Monday and it made me happy that I could do it for twelve months, so I had something to aim for. I could do it for a year or just three months; I could give up whenever I wanted to, but in a nice way, I could go as far as I needed to go. Two weeks later, I took a group to the "Make Poverty History" march in Edinburgh. That was the first thing I ever organized. It was amazing. I had to write letters; I had my own desk; I had to get transport, make T-shirts. I had to get accommodation with the "Make Poverty History" people.

'We took young people that I knew from Muirton and Fairfield, people I wanted to get involved in the YMCA as well; 'cause I'd done it, other people could. We wore white suits and made T-shirts, our own designs, and made our own massive banners. It was amazing when we got there: we walked round, everyone loved it, and when we got home, it was just like, "You're not stopping me now; I'm just going to do everything!" So then I got involved in the World Youth Congress, which was just a life-changing thing. It was delegates from all over the world, staying in Stirling. We made an outdoor classroom, out of wood and stone, and we done stone carving with them. We learned how to talk different languages, learned about other cultures and there was people from Mexico. I got really friendly with a girl called Laura, and she invited me to visit, which I didn't get to do yet but my church are going to help. It was amazing.

'I also got to go to the concert before the G8 Summit at Gleneagles – the "Final Push", it was called. I'd never been to a concert before and I was there as a ProjectScotland volunteer. There was a group of us with buckets and yellow T-shirts saying "Malawi Appeal". We had to shout it and everything... we made loads, man! It was the first time I'd come out of my shell and really shouted at people, "Put money in the bucket!" For the first time, I met other ProjectScotland volunteers, which was really good. We even got to meet Bob Geldof. Well, we saw him as he passed us, and I shouted, "Bob!" and he looked our way. He had a white top on – it was a right sort of scruffy shirt, so was his hair, but he looks quite good, eh? I like Bob, he's quite cool, even though I didn't know much about him before. My mum was watching the concert on TV and she was getting proud of me at this point. I always wanted to make my mum and dad proud of me.

'I loved being part of the campaign, seeing all the people caring about the people in Africa who are not getting what they need to live life. I find the education part hard, even though I hated school myself... Young people deserve an education and I'm quite strong pointed about it.

'I always say when I talk about ProjectScotland that if I was to make a book and put a front cover on it, it would always be, *My Second Chance in Life*, because when I was invited back in by ProjectScotland, it got me where I am now. Everything seems to be getting better. My mum and dad are getting better – they've always been really close anyway – but my little brother's up at secondary school. My mum's doing well: she's out of the house on her own, walking around on her own, she's coming to church, she's wanting to do things now, and I have made them proud of me... They don't shut up now, so it's like, every time I go in the house, they're really interested in what I do. ProjectScotland has changed everything, my whole life. After my year, I stayed on as a youth worker at the YMCA and now I am going to work with young people through the Abernethy Trust.

'I always want to work with young people – with disabilities, without disabilities, any kind of young people. I love doing it; I feel that it's a sort of gift I've got that I can go out and have a laugh with these young people and I can organize them in groups and I can have them dancing first thing in the morning when no one else can... I want to work abroad; I want to go all around the world with young people everywhere. I went to Bulgaria. I did a three-week project out there, redecorating a school in the poorest part of the country and they were really nice to us.

'When I go to schools and camps now and work with young people who have been excluded and stuff, they say to me, "You don't know nothin', man... my mum and dad take drugs and stuff and my mum's done this and my dad's done that." Well, I can relate to it. A lot of the other volunteers on the camps can't, though. I can talk to them, they can talk to me and be more open with me and more relaxed around me. I find that quite important that I can do that. When I was at camp at Easter, there was a young girl who had had her little sister die and she was really angry about it. She used to spit at us and tell us to "F-off" in the morning. She hated our guts, and we were all just Christian b-s... And there was one day when she really cracked up, and I spoke to her about it and she says, "You don't know what it feels like; my little sister died this year." And I was like, "Well, my little brother died as well," and I'm not embarrassed to share my past. So she was asking me questions about it, and I was just honest with her and she was honest with me and I helped her. She was all right for the rest of the week. She was still spitting and that, obviously, but she was more eased about that [the bereavement], which was an important thing for me 'cause I felt I'd done something.

'I've even got confidence now to be able to set up a staff meeting and be honest about my opinion. I still get stressed before I go up to speak about ProjectScotland – I feel like I'm going to lose my speech and I'm shaking and stuff, but I just tell the audience that. Then I just get all chilled out and start telling jokes and stuff... It's really good. I tell people that volunteering helped me learn about leadership, confidence, patience, tolerance and problem-solving.

'My faith is very important to me. Franny had told us his testimony and I saw what it had done for him. I got baptized a couple of years back. I was totally shocked that my mum came to the baptism 'cause she hardly left the house and she got a lift home by people in my church. We got a DVD of it – it was a full immersion – and it says at the end that my mum came and I was so excited. Having a Christian faith means I've always got somewhere else to go, and I know myself that God's got a plan for where I'm going and he's got a plan for my mum and my dad and my family, and it's just good that I've got something to fall back on, and it's only in the past two years that I've come properly to know. I like bringing other people to faith as well.

'I feel angry that I had to go through what I have and it's why I like working with young people like me. But there are lots of things I wouldn't change in the past, 'cause I wouldn't be what I am now if I hadn't had those experiences. A few years ago, I was a failure and had no future and even my friends and family thought the same. Now all that's changed. If I think about what I would want my friends to say about me [as an epitaph], it would be that I was a fighter; I always kept going.'

Paula is still very young but has astonishing wisdom and insight into her situation. At the start of our conversation, she seemed like a lost child in need of a hug but by the end, I saw her as a strong, confident young woman. I also saw how easy it is to judge troublemakers like Paula without understanding any of their stories. I have often heard people talk dismissively about teenagers getting their chance in life, failing to make the most of it, and being consigned to the scrap heap – as if it has to be that way. Paula's story reminded me of the need to be forgiving, to be prepared to give someone a second and third chance – which couldn't have happened to Paula if it hadn't been for Franny and his own journey.

It was easy to see how the education system had failed her. This was hardly surprising as she must have been impossible to teach and so disruptive. Many teachers are sympathetic to the troubled home lives of young people like Paula but don't have the time or the resources to get involved. That brief moment when she got her first award reminded me of Franny and the praise from his maths teacher that had meant so much to him. With so few moments like that, it is not surprising that Paula grew up with so little confidence and self belief. It was always easier to test the boundaries to the limit and sabotage herself before others did. It was easy to see how her anger had developed at her own family situation, although she was always so protective and loyal to her parents and brothers. She was often worried that her younger brothers would be taken into care when her mother was ill, constantly forcing her back into a less healthy home environment. However, her anger and fighting spirit have given her the determination to be independent and to develop her own life. Understanding more about Africa had clearly been important to her, and her faith has given her a structure for her life and an understanding that God has a plan for her.

I was humbled by this chain of circumstances, knowing that Cameron's death, which had prompted the start of ProjectScotland, had changed the life of a girl she would never know. It was very rewarding to know that ProjectScotland had been her turning point. It had been important for her to be given another chance by Franny and to have had the opportunity to be part of a year-long programme that paid her living expenses. However, the key for Paula was the amount of responsibility she assumed in her work with other young people, giving her the courage to make a difference. This had a dramatic impact on her own self-belief and confidence, as is evident when she said, 'I now know I can change things for myself and for others too, and it feels great.'

7

BOB GELDOF

I've faced plenty of challenges in life, but interviewing Bob Geldof was one I didn't particularly look forward to. I knew some previous interviewers had received a mixed response, and I understood that getting on the wrong side of him could be an alarming experience. He clearly does not suffer fools, and has been known to meet any kind of intrusive, tabloid-style questioning with fiery outbursts. At the same time, his courage, decency and passion for justice shine through in his books and interviews, as much as his wit and intelligence. I was also amused that Paula Lowther had found him 'quite cool' when he made a brief appearance in her life. Paula and Bob seemed to have turned their anger at their upbringing and their fighting spirit into something that could be used for the good of others.

I was fascinated by his story. Having just visited Rwanda, I am even more aware of the suffering in Africa and, like many, overwhelmed by the vast scale of it. Why was Bob the one who responded with such alacrity and anger to the images of starving children in Ethiopia in the 1980s? Gordon Brown was moved by his daughter's death to do more for children across the world who die needlessly, but he was a politician, not a musician. Bob has spoken of Africa as a place that 'feels like... going home', an intriguing statement for an Irish-born star.

I met him the morning after his birthday in the London office of his record company, Universal Music. I heard the attractive Irish lilt before I saw him, as he chatted amiably with staff outside the meeting room. Minutes later, he stood in the doorway, looked me up and down and complimented me on the way I looked, leaving me flustered and charmed in equal measure. He was taller than I expected and cleaner, in spite of admitting to having been 'on the razzle' the night before. His outfit of jeans, striped jumper, gold chain, wild hair and blue duffel coat fitted the pop star image, even if he now had a more famous role on the world stage. Despite the warmth of the room, he remained curled up inside this coat throughout the interview, using it like some kind of security blanket.

I wanted, quite simply, to understand Bob's turning point, to know what turned a veteran rock star into a respected voice in global politics. I knew already that his personal history had prepared him for upheaval and sudden changes of direction. Born in 1951, he was brought up just outside Dublin by his father, a travelling salesman, having suffered the 'unbearable loss' of his mother to a brain haemorrhage when he was seven. He often speaks about the poverty and loneliness of that time and his intense dislike of school and the church. After a variety of dismal jobs, he enjoyed a successful stint as a music reporter in Canada before being deported. On his return to Ireland, he formed the punk-rock band The Boomtown Rats, and for some years was an internationally successful performer and, briefly, an actor in the film *The Wall*. He also married the well-known TV presenter Paula Yates and had three daughters with her. Some years later, he suffered the torment of losing her to the pop star Michael Hutchence, followed by their subsequent tragic deaths, and his high-profile adoption of their daughter, Tiger Lily.

It was in late 1984, while his music career was falling apart, that Bob watched the story of the drought victims of the Ethiopian famine on the news. At that moment, his life changed forever. Within a year, he had written and produced the Band Aid single 'Do They Know It's Christmas?' and organized the

Live Aid concerts, the biggest TV event in history, raising over £100 million for Africa and galvanizing the world into action. He received an honorary knighthood for that work in 1986. In 2005, he produced the Live 8 concerts in five countries to raise awareness of issues in Africa ahead of the G8 summit in Scotland, and successfully persuaded the world leaders to double aid to $50 billion for Africa's poor. The consequences of his turning point are plain for everyone to see. But I was interested in the 'why'. Why respond to the images of the Ethiopian famine and not some other cause? What had been happening in his own life to ready him for that personal transition?

'Well, to me it's all logical. I don't think it was some eureka moment... like I just watched telly and then suddenly decided to change my entire life. But circumstances dictated that I happened to be in that place at that time, and that I was alert to those sorts of things because of my upbringing.

'When I was very young, the things that interested me were reading and listening to the radio because we didn't have telly. I wasn't interested in school or sport, just the sport of politics. I did the anti-apartheid thing when I was thirteen, and I worked with the Simon community aged fifteen and sixteen, going round Dublin all night with flasks of soup for the homeless. I was alert to that sort of thing. And when I left school, I lived amongst those sorts of people for many years, because I just had crap jobs.

'It sounds so clichéd, but a turning point came when my mother died when I was about seven. While you're a child, it doesn't really impact upon you, but you are left with a sense of unfairness, without "gilding the lily" here. If you look at people who have lost a parent very young, they don't trust authority. If the people you trust bail out on you by dying or whatever, then why should you trust anything any other adults say? You end up kicking against this and that – and school was more of the same.

'When my mother died, it felt like the world caving in. I remember the night before it happened – the evening light and sitting in the bay window with her and a friend, then going to bed and having a quick cuddle with her. My dad was there, so it was probably a weekend, because he was away during the week. I was sharing a bedroom with my sister, and her mate Olivia was over and they were going to have a midnight feast. I asked them to wake me so I could join in, and I did wake up in the middle of the night but they told me to go back to sleep as it wasn't midnight yet. I said, "I can hear you crying," but they said, "No, we're laughing," so I went back to sleep. When I woke up the next morning, the house was full of noise. But it was a hushed noise, I remember that, and then my father comes up and very bluntly and correctly tells me that my mum died last night. He started crying, and as a result, I started crying. I didn't cry 'cause of the news that my mother was dead, but it was so out of the blue, you know, there was no warning or lingering illness… just BANG. But what freaked me out was my dad crying. I'd never seen a man cry and so I felt I was expected to cry too.

'Then I was dispatched by my elder sister, who was about seventeen, across the road to a little girl with the unlikely name of Jackie Kennedy and with all the glamour that attaches to that particular appellation. I got out the white Nazi helmet that we had in the house – my father had painted it white to "exorcize the ghosts" – and I went over to her place. Then I was packed off to stay with some people, as in those days children didn't go to funerals. But I remember going to see the "Kings of Comedy" with Buster Keaton and Charlie Chaplin, then going back to school and the boys keeping a distance and the priests, who were usually a pain, being over-solicitous, which I quite enjoyed. And that was it. There was no moment of clarity… that this was forever, that this person we spent our lives with was gone forever. But after that it just got crap, everything got crap, our family sort of atomized.

'It's unbearable to be that small and to have to take care of yourself. At the time, you just get on with it and it becomes routine to shop, to cook and to get the coal from the basement to light the fire 'cause there's no central heating. It's crap coming home alone – it's always a dark November evening in my head – to that big empty old house as my sisters were never there. On one occasion, I got ill and couldn't get up, and it was three days before my sister realized I was upstairs. But it didn't bother me, as I felt like s**t. There's an element of self-pity creeping in as I say this, but not pity for now. For then. I must've been a bit fed up.'

More than a bit fed up, I thought, as I watched him hunching down further into his protective duffel coat. As a mother, I found it very hard to listen to Bob speak about this and, much as he might try to suggest it wasn't so bad at the time, I could see now where his anger came from, and why he might so easily empathize with the loss and suffering of children in Africa. Journalists have expressed amazement that he should have wished to adopt the daughter of his ex-wife and her lover, but now I was speaking to him, it seemed obvious that there could be no other way for him to respond. Was it, I wondered, on a very basic level, his own experience of hardship that gave him a social conscience?

'Ireland was an extremely poor country with very few jobs. I left school with no qualifications and groped my way around the world. At one point I was living on the streets of London. It didn't bother me because I was young and I could get a sleeping bag and a sponge mattress in the crypt at High Holborn or I slept at Gatwick Airport for a while. But all the time, I was alert and watching people. Eventually I ended up doing something I liked in Canada and then my life started. When it came to writing songs for The Boomtown Rats, they were always about things, you know? They weren't about nothing. They were about things that mattered to me. I wrote "Rat Trap" while I was working in the abattoir in Dublin about a guy called Paul – who becomes Billy in the song. It was about the hopelessness of his situation, trapped in this perennial poverty, where there's no getting out, and even his girlfriend calls him "loser". "I Don't Like Mondays" was about a girl in America who leaned out of her bedroom window with a gun and started shooting schoolchildren, bizarrely telling this journalist who spoke to her that she just didn't like Mondays. I was just trying to get my head round it.

'When I think back to the TV reports of starving children in Ethiopia, I realize I may have been more alert than another person simply because of my background. But you've got to understand the moment. Having been this very successful band, The Boomtown Rats, we were now on the downward slide. We'd become past our sell-by date, and while I agree that turnover has to happen in pop music terms, intellectually it's very hard to accept. Especially when you think you're still doing stuff that creatively is at least as good as what you were doing before. I had a nine-month-old baby now – that's significant, because I was very worried about what was going to happen to me and my wife Paula and baby Fifi. I was still young. I thought, jeez, that's it, it's over, that amazing part of my life, which didn't seem that amazing when I was doing it. And I turned on the six o'clock news. And in itself, that could only have happened then. If the famine had been going on in 1979, when we were still successful, we'd have been on tour or something and I'd never have seen it. But we weren't doing particularly well, so I was at home. There were no interviews, no recordings, the last record wasn't selling and I was worried. I turned on the news and I remember Fifi being cuddled up against me on the sofa and Paula on my other side and we saw this devastatingly brilliant, now very famous, piece of news reporting. I remember it very well to this day… the images of that report and the metaphors that were brilliantly played with, though I don't think Michael Buerk understood what he was doing. He was shocked by what he saw and you could clearly see that and hear it. The brevity of the words hung in the silence and his outrage reverberated around. Mohammed Amin's camera work was ruthless and brilliant and so it was polemic, much more than it was reporting.

'It may as well have had "For The Attention Of Bob Geldof" on it, for the mood I was in, the time of day, the condition of my life – new family, no future, best part of my life over, evening, October – everything pushing above and in me, I guess. Here I was with a little baby, and here I was seeing all these mothers and fathers and children absolutely no different to us; I really saw no difference. I didn't see it as though it was another planet, removed from us just because they were wearing togas.'

As Bob spoke, his body language changed and I began to see the Geldof that politicians must sometimes fear to deal with. He exuded real passion for his subject and real determination to be heard. He gesticulated and jabbed at the air, ensuring I never dared to interrupt the flow.

'It is important to remember the times we were in, too. In 1984, people were getting really outraged by the Common Agricultural Policy, that they were paying tax to grow surplus food. They then paid tax to store it and paid tax to destroy it, while not that many miles south of Europe, 30 million people were dying of starvation. That was the immediate connection I made with what I saw on Buerk's report, because the next day I decided that to die of want in a world of surplus is not only intellectually absurd, it's morally repulsive. And I knew that putting a quid in the box just wasn't enough in the face of this, given the huge disparity between our world and theirs. I thought at first I would write a song and make around seventy grand. And because The Boomtown Rats weren't having hits, the logic was to use my mates from the ten years I'd spent in rock 'n' roll, and rising young bands like U2, to perform "Do They Know It's Christmas?"

'Paula had cried watching the film and had to leave halfway through as she was too distressed. The next morning, she had to leave for Newcastle with Fifi to do the filming for *The Tube* with Jools Holland. Before she went, she left a note on the fridge saying that anyone who visited the house had to put five quid in this shoebox she'd stuck on the kitchen table. When I saw that, it really, really alerted my outrage and that's what made me decide to write a song. I was sitting by myself having coffee with that note on the fridge, and there was a phone on the coffee table, so I just reached for it and called Newcastle and spoke to Paula. I asked who was on the show that night and she said Midge Ure was there. We knew Midge, like all the other new kids in the business, like Duran Duran and Spandau Ballet. They would come to visit our house in Kent and they knew Paula from *The Tube*, which was the hip thing in TV back then. I was a bit shamefaced suggesting "hip" bands should play my song when I wasn't doing well, so when I called Midge, I started by suggesting we cover some old standard to raise money. But he disagreed and said I should write a song. I said, "I don't have any," so he said, "I'll do something, you do something, and let's see if anything comes." That validation, him just assuming I was a songwriter and musician, regardless of whether I was having hits at that time, was clearly what I wanted to hear, but I hadn't wanted to suggest it. So off I went. I knocked off "Do They Know It's Christmas?" in a taxi on my way to see a sick friend.'

I was intrigued by his mention of the validation he'd received from fellow musician Midge Ure. It was clear from everything I'd read that Bob has many insecurities, in spite of his outward confidence, perhaps something stemming from his childhood and the lack of adult approval. He never seems comfortable with the kind of adulation and notions of sainthood surrounding his work in Africa – perhaps because he feels unworthy of it.

'No, I can't stand that. I think fairly strategically, you know. I don't engage in gestural politics. I'm not interested in going on protest marches and waving banners because I don't think anything is achieved except to create the lobby, but where's the plan you're hoping to get implemented? You must have that. You must have truly achievable aims. I've also got a feel for the moment – that's how I managed to write hit songs. In 1984, Britain was doing pretty well, but we were engaged in this very Eighties, "Greed is Good" thing. I never minded the idea of a kid being eighteen and earning a fortune and driving around in a Porsche and red braces looking like a twat – good luck to you, dude – but it can't stop there; you can do something with the stuff you've got. Maybe there are other people that you can help along the way. In Britain, there was clearly a breakdown of some sort, and in that vacuum Band Aid thrived. If you pro rata'd it, the greatest Band Aid contributions came out of the mining villages. That was because this was the era of the miners' strikes, and they were going through crap, just like I was when I saw the Buerk thing. The response of the cities was also great, and if you remember, Fortnum and Mason had the Band Aid single all over the shop, with queues down the street, and butchers in Plymouth were selling it beside the turkeys and ducks for Christmas. It was a phenomenon. It seemed to fill that vacuum where we were uneasy about what we'd become and unsure of the future, but pretty certain things had to move forward. We were becoming aware of the Common Agricultural Policy and its economic aberrations and absurdities, as well as its faulty morals. It was no campaign, it was no great rallying call, it wasn't planned, but as I said, I think strategically. I thought we'd get 72 grand if we did the song, but 8 million later, after I'd cracked on and on about what we had to do, I realized there was no way I could suddenly say, "There's 8 million now, so I'm going to f**k off." Here was this massive wellspring of opinion saying, "Let's do this thing," so I went to Africa and saw what was going on, but that wasn't enough. I had to do something else, and that ended up as the Live Aid concert.

'Twenty years later, you get to this government, some of whose opinions were formed by those events when they were young men, just beginning their careers in politics. They saw this practical application of a political idea – using the tools of marketing in effect – I think they were very influenced by it. I've talked to Gordon [Brown] and I've talked to Tony [Blair] about it and clearly they saw this. So when they got to be in power, it was very logical that I would go to them and say that all those supporters are still with us, you know, we've built this into a focused lobby, so let's now try and take that to its logical and political conclusion. That's what the plan for the G8 summit at Gleneagles and Live 8 was. I made a TV series on Africa to try to explain the concept specifically to the UK, to popularize the Gleneagles and the Commission for Africa agenda.'

I wondered whether his interest in Africa ever became too all-consuming, knowing from my own experience how easy it can be for children to make you feel guilty for being away from them. I suspected he must be feeling frustrated by endless stories of the antics of his teenage daughters and I assumed his skills as a father were probably being questioned by the kind of journalist he loathed. I suggested his children would be very proud of what he was doing, but he was quick to tell me that 'They couldn't give a f**k!' Even so, he was keen to defend his role as a hands-on father, explaining that he keeps foreign trips on a tight schedule to avoid being away too long.

'I work out of the house, just using the sitting room and my mobile while the kids are at school. If I'm out, I'll be back at six. Most days I'm in when they come home, and Jeanne (his long-term partner) is there all the time. I see my children more than most dads with normal jobs do. And if it came down to a choice between any of the things I do and them – it would be them, without any doubt.'

From noticing the starving children when he was a new parent in 1984 to struggling with the demands of a busy family now, fatherhood looms large in his personality. I wondered what other elements were there too. He continually mentions religion in his books – in a variety of contexts, from his dislike of the Catholic Church in Ireland, to the remarkable work of missionaries in Africa and his respect for Mother Theresa, whom he admires for her deft manipulation of the media and her total selflessness. Religion is significant for him – yet he refers to himself firmly, and perplexingly, as a lapsed unbeliever and an atheist and considers his work in Africa to be a natural consequence of being an ordinary human, not some faith in the supernatural.

'I am an atheist and I find a great comfort in the lack of God, because it's good fun knowing that it's wholly explicable and nonsensical, and there is a great comfort in knowing that it's all over at the end. People say, if there's no God, there's no morality, but that's absolutely ridiculous. Morality, this notion, this philosophical idea of morality, is hard-wired. I believe it's simply a social function. If we harmed each other in the early days of humanity, when there were very few of us, we were not going to survive. You can see that in some African societies, where they developed in a particular way because of environmental conditions. You get small groups of travelling people leading a nomadic life in harsh conditions – so they have this view that even if you've only got a little bit, you must share it or else society collapses. And if you harm anyone in that little group, the group is weaker and therefore you're weaker, so it's all self-evident.'

With typical modesty, he seemed to be saying that he'd only done what was natural and obvious for anyone to do. But I still felt there might be some spiritual element to his thinking. In his autobiography *Is That It?* he mentioned speaking to his dead mother in times of stress during the Live Aid concert. He also referred to a kind of divine providence, a sense that things just fell into place for him as he asked people to help with Band

Aid and then began to organize the Live Aid concerts. Having felt myself that Cameron's life and death, and continuing presence, had shaped my own journey, I could relate strongly to that idea. But I couldn't understand how it applied if you didn't have a faith.

'When you're a child and you're overwrought and desperate, you look for help. I remember when I was in serious trouble in school and at home, and terrified of my dad at that point, I would pray to my mother to intercede. I wouldn't physically pray, but I'd panic and turn to a supernatural option in the form of my dead mother. She wasn't a vivid presence, but sometimes she would scare me. I'd be sitting in the basement kitchen reading, with my feet in the gas oven because I couldn't be arsed going up and lighting the fire in the big living room. I'd be tilted back in the kitchen chair and I'd purposely stay focused on my book and I'd just stay looking 'cause I was afraid that if I looked up at the window I'd see her face. But that's a young boy's panic. I was in a permanent state of panic and fear, you know, about what was happening to me.

'During Live Aid, things happened which were coincidental. There is a quote I often use, sent to me in a letter, by a Scottish mountaineer called W. H. Murray. He says that once you've definitely committed yourself, providence moves too. That's a good word, providence, because he's not appealing to the divine or the spiritual. But as a result of any act of initiative or creation, things happen that no man could have dreamt of – material things come your way, meetings occur – I can't remember the quote exactly, but that's precisely what happened to me. He ends the quote by paraphrasing Goethe: "Whatever you can do or dream you can, begin it. Boldness has genius, power and magic in it." And you know, it's true, even my sister getting well in Lourdes [having been diagnosed with terminal cancer]. I absolutely believe that there are things that just happen. I mean we have truly no understanding of the physical world, none whatsoever. We scratch at the surface of this reality we perceive, which may or may not exist, and in fact probably doesn't. We invent a geezer with a beard and a Star Trek language for this supreme being, lord of the universe. It's so improbably stupid, but I don't mind if people believe it, obviously, and I'm not being patronizing. I can't stand atheist fundamentalists any more than I can stand the others. But the intellectual f***ing knots you have to tie yourself into to believe in God in the first place, even in standard religions, are so LUDICROUS!'

I wanted to return to Bob's idea of death, without an afterlife, being a 'great comfort'. It reminded me that in a previous interview, he'd spoken of the oblivion of death being a welcome prospect. But that didn't sit well with his commitment to saving lives in Africa. Why bother, if death is a welcome thing?

'I don't welcome death… I'd welcome it if my life was s**t and, you know, I'm a miserable f***er at the best of times, but again that's a product of what happened. I don't go around like those cartoons you see – with the weeping cloud over my head – but I do get very nervy and edgy during the twilight hours and autumn afternoons and I have to turn on a lot of lights. I tend not to be able to see very well in it, but at the same time it's quite good for writing songs. When I'm cosy with Jeanne and the kids at that time of day, I feel really great. I would regret dying but I don't fear age. My dad's in his nineties and my uncle was ninety-four when he died. But he worked every day, drove 20 miles to work, 20 miles back until he died. My dad is reporting back from the Front Line [of old age] you know; objectively I mean it's fantastic, but he is also so annoyed with the pain of it and the incontinence. I just hope I'm firing on those sort of intellectual cylinders at his age.'

He hadn't entirely answered my question but I felt pretty sure that Bob had no love for oblivion, and no desire to send other people there either. With all this talk of endings, I wondered whether he could ever see an end to his work in Africa. Would he ever reach a point where he felt he'd done enough – or would he remain driven for the rest of his life?

'Well there must be plateaus, such as Live 8, when you set out goals and you say, "I think we can get to here, then we can get to there, then we can get to there." And once you arrive at that point, people feel a sense of achievement, and that's great. If you don't have set goals, terrible cynicism sets in and the political process cannot afford cynicism. So the next part of the plan was the Commission for Africa, persuading Tony Blair to do a political Band Aid in effect, gathering the powers that be and enabling them to sign off on this plan to reduce poverty. Will it all be done? No, but a good proportion of it will be done and already you've seen millions more children in school, people kept alive during droughts and a free national health service in Zambia, for example. It has to work, because if it didn't the cost to all the politicians involved would be huge. Why should the voters believe anything again?'

Like Mother Theresa, whom he'd met, I sensed that there was a shrewd politician inside Bob Geldof. I wondered how this side of him got on with the angry agitator and the creative musician.

'The reality for me is that I divide my life fairly evenly between business, music, the family and the political stuff, and they all have a function. I do the politics for my head. I do the business for my stomach. I do the music for my soul. And I do my family for my heart.'

Politics for his head? Somehow, I doubted that it was just an intellectual exercise. There's an angry streak that runs through Bob Geldof – it's what the media focuses on, often to the exclusion of all else, but it's an undeniable part of him. The horror and misery he witnessed in Africa made him angry and surely it was that which powered his first steps towards change.

'Yeah, it is the motor although it's actually less profound than anger. Rather pathetically, it's more irascibility and irritability.

It's like things shouldn't be like this and they don't have to be like this and that's a f***ing irritation with me. I do tend to look at an issue and very quickly break it down into exactly what's wrong and say, "That doesn't have to be like that, that really doesn't." You're always seeing me on TV saying, "It doesn't have to be like that." The focus can be on my not-very-amenable personality, but that's all right, so long as we debate.

'The thing I also say a lot is "Why not make a go of it?" Given what I believe, it seems to me that it's so fantastically odd that the conscious individual personality called "Bob" exists for a snap of time – and that construct probably doesn't really exist, but it's the only way we can gather our wits in this universe… But, given that it's all essentially purposeless, why not make a go of it? Why be supine in the face of life? It's not going to happen again.

'I once spoke to the Dalai Lama in a monastery in Budapest and I told him, "I don't want to come back as a f***ing leg of a kitchen table or a parrot or something," and he said, "Well too bad, you're going to have to," and I said, "I don't, it's the most ridiculous f***ing thing to believe in ever," and he said, "We've proof," and I said, "You've no proof. You've no proof at all; you just believe that to be so… We are part of the organic structure of the universe, and in time, it all decays, everything goes, the lot. Show me one single thing that exists in a future realm – grass goes, sheep go, your parrot goes." And he says, "Well, too bad for you then." '

I thought, but didn't say, that it must have been a tough day for the Dalai Lama. But when he wasn't challenging world spiritual leaders, I could see that Bob's 'carpe diem' philosophy had its strengths. By not believing in an afterlife or a world beyond, all the focus went on to what could be achieved in the here and now.

'The idea is that you utilize whatever it is you've got to its utmost, without hurting anyone else. And you know, some individuals are capable of more than others and some less than others, and you just have to push that experiment-that's-you right to its limits, to the point of exhaustion, where you're frightened, where failure is this gaping chasm ahead of you.'

So had a fear of failure motivated him as much as the desire to correct the world? Was that why, with worries about his continuing musical career looming, he'd first embarked on a new path as an activist? Bob seemed not to feel that this had played any larger part in his life than in anyone else's.

'All lives end in failure. It's over, and I don't mean that in a nasty way; I mean it just is. I'll regret that it's all gone and I've been f***ing gloomy throughout most of it, but the things I've seen and my friends and my family and the stuff I've been through are f***ing amazing. I'll just regret that it's over. But at the same time, I don't want to live until my nineties like my dad and feeling that he can't do the stuff he wants to.'

His philosophy seemed to be that life was somewhat absurd and random, but at the same time that meant we had to push ourselves to achieve things, perhaps as the only useful thing we could do. I found it fascinating, but full of contradictions, and my mind boggled at the idea that he could find it comforting. But then again, perhaps he didn't find it comforting – and perhaps that was why Bob Geldof was who he was. I felt sad when I heard his views on the end of life – sad that he didn't have the comfort of believing he would meet his loved ones again. I remembered sitting with Cameron's mother Blyth on a beach, the summer after her death. She was struggling to control her tears in front of Flora, my five-year-old daughter, who suddenly turned to her and said, 'Don't be sad. You'll see Cameron again in heaven; she'll be having tea with my great-grandma.' Blyth turned to me and said that was what kept her going, knowing she would see Cameron again one day and sensing that she was always with her. I wondered how this contradictory, brilliant man I was interviewing now had coped with his losses and how he'd explained Paula's death to his daughters – although it didn't seem appropriate to ask outright. I settled for asking what he made of Blyth's words to me on that beach.

'She's not gonna meet her again. She died because she was ill or she was in an accident and there is no karmic Rag, Tag and Bobtail. She just f***ing died, and so the conscious identity of that girl had that span and it's f***ing awful because her mother will be destroyed by that. I don't see how you come back from the loss of a child; I don't see how because they're the repository of everything human. It's all the hope, all the good stuff, all the future, all possible love goes into these things, you know, human beings are... great.'

Swearing and railing against the universe, in between declaring that humans were great – it seemed very typically Bob Geldof, and at that moment, we were interrupted and the interview was over. I was filled with admiration for a man who had turned a rough start in life and the first turning point of his mother's death into the most remarkable service for others. I felt sure that his mother knew how he'd turned out – and I wished he felt the same. If I had to write an epitaph for him, I would probably use his phrase 'It doesn't have to be like that', which sums him up so well and reflects his other turning point – the moment when he watched coverage of the Ethiopian famine on TV and was angered and appalled by what he saw.

It was only later that his final remarks about Cameron started to haunt me. Some of his arguments in favour of atheism were very articulate, and I could see how someone who had experienced childhood bereavement, and then witnessed the appalling poverty and inhumanity of an African famine, could doubt the idea of an all-loving, all-powerful God. But I wondered how he coped with the absence. Plainly he hadn't fallen apart after his mother's death, or the waning of his pop career, or any of the other difficulties that happened to him. But he seemed angry at this random, pointless universe he believed himself to live in. And at the same time, he could see faith only as an illusion – not as something sustaining, creative and helpful. He was wrong about Cameron's mother: she has not been destroyed by what has happened. The pain may never leave her, but she has adjusted to a life without Cameron, and her faith has kept her strong. But perhaps, in a curious way, Bob needs his own lack of spiritual comfort to do what he does. Perhaps without it he would be less angry, less restless, less driven to get things done.

8

DIANE IRABARUTA

Not long ago I met and got to know someone very special, someone who actually came from the kind of impossible circumstances that so angered Bob Geldof. I was late for a wedding in my local church, Holy Trinity, in St Andrews and had to take a pew close to the back. After an exhausting meeting in Edinburgh, I had considered missing the wedding completely but did not want to let my friends down. Life would be different and perhaps a bit simpler if I had not made it, but neither would it be as blessed. That chance meeting led me to discover the remarkable country of Rwanda and took me another step on my journey.

A young African girl arrived in the pew behind me and, without looking round, I sensed she was in some distress. She slipped away from the church early but stayed in my mind over the next two days. When she appeared at our Sunday service, I was able to meet her properly. She explained that she was from Rwanda and was working as an intern at our local five-star hotel.

Diane Irabaruta had lost her entire family in the genocide of 1994, when she was only thirteen. She had come a long way since then, with her tremendous courage and determination, but was struggling emotionally at the time I met her. She was not sleeping well and had come to the church for help. Her life was to be changed by the loving response she received from our minister, Rory Macleod, and from friends who offered her a home and loving care.

As she told me some of her story, I realized how little I knew about events that had happened in that distant part of the world. Focusing on building my career had meant that, apart from a vague awareness of African issues (thanks to Bob Geldof), the genocide was to me just one of many stories of misery that seemed to be part of life for many Africans. Diane was to change my perception and to provide a new dimension to my faith and understanding of God.

This is not the place for a history of Rwanda, but there is little doubt that the genocide was the direct result of terrible colonial policies in the twentieth century which led to an ethnic division in the country between the Hutu and Tutsi people. Ultimately, the use of ID cards to define people on ethnic lines was the key to the success of the genocide. Like Paul Kagame, the current President of Rwanda, Diane's parents had been forced to flee to Uganda in 1960 with many other Tutsis after the Hutus took control. Kagame had led the invasion by the RPF (Rwandan Patriotic Front) to try to return his people to the country they loved in 1990. As a power-sharing agreement with the Hutu authorities in the capital of Kigali began to falter, tensions arose and the dangerous Hutu *interhamwe* militia groups started to form. The death of the Hutu president in a plane crash became the rallying call for the genocide to start, and within a few months over a million people had been brutally massacred while the UN and the Western world failed to intervene. Both President Clinton and Tony Blair have given a good deal of their time to Rwanda, perhaps as a form of atonement. But we are all implicated in the failure to get involved, ignoring the desperate pleas for help. It is still a poor country, where most people live in mud houses on barely more than a dollar a day, suffering from a massive number of people who were orphaned in the genocide or lost parents to Aids or malaria. Thirteen per cent of households are run by children.

Diane had been keen for my family to visit her in Rwanda

after her return, and an opportunity arose for me to go there in November 2008. I still found it hard to relate the girl I knew to the stories she told or to the movies we saw telling the Rwanda story. One night in Scotland she had shown us the film *Shooting Dogs*, based on a true story of a massacre of 2,500 Tutsis at a high school in Kigali run by priests and abandoned by UN soldiers. As my husband and I sat there wiping tears from our eyes, Diane remained quiet and almost impassive, simply mentioning that a member of her family had died there. It seemed that she was keeping too much inside, and, accustomed to our world of stress disorders and therapy as a solution, I longed to see whether I could help. The visit seemed a good idea.

I travelled to the capital, Kigali, with her charming landlord from her stay in St Andrews, the man she came to call 'Uncle' John Rankin, and we met up with my friend Karyn Purvis, part of an American team working with orphanages there. There were instances of concern as tensions flared in the neighbouring Congo, but we found a country of incredible beauty and charm. Lush and abundant countryside, rare wildlife, such as the mountain gorillas, and the constant kindness of the people gave us moments of real joy. It is impossible to forget, however, that its greatest fame comes from its suffering. In every village there is a memorial or sign to the genocide, and the government is determined that people should move on but also never forget as a way of ensuring it never happens again. Mass graves are still being found everywhere, and the Genocide Museum in Kigali, the site of one such grave for 250,000 people, provides many poignant reminders of the suffering, particularly of the children who were targeted first. I was drawn to photographs of children the same age as mine: one label read 'Francine Muregezi, age twelve, favourite food, egg and chips, loves swimming, hacked to death by machete'. Shocking news footage of bloated bodies of innocent children lying by the roadside and floating down rivers reminded me of what I had managed to ignore.

The hardest part of our trip was a visit to the church compound at Nyamata where 10,000 people had died in one terrible massacre. Our guide, the gentle and softly spoken Charles Mugabe, had been nine at the time and survived, I imagine, by being buried under so many bodies. It was terrible to discover that the priests had abandoned everyone to their fate, having colluded with the government to ensure people all fled to one place and were therefore easier to kill.

We walked quietly through the battered and bullet-ridden entrance to find a simple church with stone benches piled high with thousands and thousands of items of clothing, taken from the victims. The altar cloth is still bloodstained, and a machete and rosary beads are the symbolic mementoes on the altar table. Our guide told us that the altar was the place where they cut open the pregnant women to tear their babies from them, and the bloodstained wall at the back was where they battered children to death. You don't think things can get much worse until you head for the underground rooms where battered and bullet-ridden skulls and bones of adults and children lie alongside the few coffins for those families who were able to be identified. One coffin stood symbolically apart and perhaps was the ultimate symbol of the utter darkness that came over the country (anyone there in those days talks of the Devil himself being at large). The guide told us it contained a woman who had had one spear forced vertically up through her body and another through her chest and through the baby on her back. The image of Christ on the cross came to my mind in that terrible moment. John and I could barely speak and all I could manage to say to the guide as we left was 'I'm so sorry.'

The suffering of children like Diane has been imprinted on my mind now, and I am beginning to grasp how much courage and determination it takes to move on with life after such a terrible experience. The whole country had experienced an unimaginably awful turning point in its history and had the choice to collapse and die or to come back stronger. Diane was determined to show me the new Rwanda, full of impressive new buildings, coffee shops and hotels. She reflected the feelings of a very optimistic, clean and well-organized country that wanted the world to see it as a model for a new Africa.

I met with Diane to interview her in a hotel room in Kigali, after she had finished work for the day. She was so different from the girl I had first met in the church in St Andrews. She looked confident, elegant and professional in her smart white jacket, black trousers, simple jewellery and chic hairstyle. She seemed determined to succeed in life and move on from the past. She was not keen to say a great deal about what had happened to her, but I found her dignified, simple and unemotional descriptions almost more poignant. She grew up speaking French so occasionally would struggle with words and, like many Africans, had an exaggerated politeness, repeating phrases like 'if I may say' throughout the conversation. I simply asked her to tell me her story and how she had survived the genocide and rebuilt her life.

'I was born in August 1980. My parents were in exile in Kampala at that time. When I was three years old my father, Rutembesa Stratton, who was a successful businessman there, was taken from our home and killed by the Ugandan government. This was during President Obote's rule, and many Rwandans were being accused of helping the rebels in Uganda, led by their current president, Museveni. My mother's family were still living in Rwanda so she came back here and got remarried to another man. Her name was Marie Jeanne. They had two girls together, but then he died as a result of sickness. My mother gave us so much; we grew up with so much love and she really spoiled us. I remember she always did her best to give us the best education, if I may say, we never missed anything. She was very strong; she went through a lot losing two husbands but people never knew. She was always hard-working; she never liked to fail.

'We grew up in a big house in Kigali with my grandparents. My mother used to work at the high school as a lecturer. Later she ran her own business. When I was eight years old, my grandfather died. He had been jailed for twenty-three years and had only recently been released. He had been part of the monarchy of Rwanda, and when things changed he was imprisoned. I still had my grandmother. I grew up in a lovely family. We never had a father but our mother prayed and it was like we had a Father, and the place where we were staying, it was like a family residential area. It had aunties, uncles and cousins around us. So, in 1990, when the RPF invasion began, my mother was jailed for a short time, accused of being part of the RPF. When she came home, they stopped everything for her. She used to travel and go to Europe when she was a businesswoman, but they took her passport away. So she stayed here and worked for a Canadian company, and then the genocide began in 1994. We lived in this residential area where many of the victims were and where everyone was killed... everyone... yes, the whole family... no one survived.

'When the genocide first began, we stayed in our area. We were with the family, gathering together, and they said maybe these young girls can go to another place so they will be safe. My sisters Denise and Dati were too young, aged nine and seven, to go, but there were cousins with me. We went actually to a neighbour's house to hide there first, but when we arrived there the militias came and attacked us, so we had to run from Kigali to Butare in the south, which took a night and a day. We were so tired, but it was a bad situation and we had no choice but to go by foot. We can't explain how we escaped but we managed to. We passed through forest, kind of hidden places. We didn't pass to the main road. We got to some nuns at a convent in Butare and stayed there for two months.

'We heard nothing from my family, but we were treated really well, compared to the situation that was there. When we were there some people came, the same people – the militia – and they killed everyone who was there together but myself and two other girls. They left us behind. One soldier asked, "Why are you here?" I say, "I came here to be with my auntie, who was a nun." But I was lying; I didn't have any auntie there. So they took me out from the group and two other girls who were permanently staying in that place. So the rest of the people, they took them and they killed them, even my cousins. After three weeks there was an organization called Terre des Hommes who were going around picking up kids who were left, survivors, and they took us to Burundi. I went with them. It was on 2nd of July and it was on the 3rd, if I may say, that the RPF took over Kigali and Rwanda and the genocide came to an end. It was on the 4th of July that I arrived in Burundi and found my Aunt Regine and I stayed with her for two months.

'After that I came back to Rwanda, because now the country was free. I went to look for my family, but no one was there and they told me everyone was killed… and not only the house… like the whole residential area was gone; no one was there. It was like the thing [the massacre] you saw at Nyamata. I don't know exactly what happened to my mother and sisters, but they showed us the place where had they put them, where they held people. You can't find someone individually and I didn't even want to… It was a group of people who killed them… We did an official burial but there is no grave… The government has official places, and the country remembers the genocide for a week every year.

'I remember I felt like everything was gone, and I felt like nothing will make me happy anymore… But one day I just decided to go on with my life. I think it was partly my childhood and remembering my mother that gave me the strength, because I said if I'm going to stay here, cry everyday, tell everyone how unhappy I am, it's not going to help me, so I just decided to look forward. I went to high school until I was nineteen, and then I got a job as manager of a hair salon for four years. I always asked God to give me a better education, and then I got a scholarship and I was really blessed because I went to a University of Technology in Cape Town. It was good and I got nice internships like the one in St Andrews, and now I am Hospitality Director at the State House for the President and First Lady in Kigali.

'My relationship with God has changed. From 1994 until 2003, I never used to go to church. I was born Roman Catholic. I just maybe said a prayer before I went to sleep, things like that. I never really knew God, the real God. So in 2004, when I went to South Africa, that's when I started to pray, like praying on my own, and I met someone at university and she told me about Jesus and praying and the way to get healing. I started to go to the Pentecostal church and there I received Jesus as my saviour. Since that time, that's when I felt like something is changing in my life. Like faith, like if you can trust Jesus you can go everywhere, and I started really to pray hard and until now, the only thing I am afraid of is Jesus. Then I came to St Andrews and I met all of you and that changed my life. I felt like I was in another world where people can smile and love and care.'

Diane put great emphasis on those words 'love' and 'care', and it seemed to me that in her determination to be independent and move on with her life, it was hard for her to feel loved and cared for. As she spoke, she seemed to me to become the child again, rather than the businesswoman. She described how she had stayed with an auntie for a while in Rwanda, but it seemed to be a close family friend who had done the most for her. I knew how important the church had become for her, and when in Rwanda I had tried to find out more about what was happening. A Scottish minister, Callum Henderson, has written movingly of remarkable reconciliation meetings in churches between people who lost their families and the murderers responsible, which he would describe as relying completely on God's grace. A pastor in Rwanda described these moments simply as another of God's miracles and said that it was essential for the victim to find a way to forgive although never to forget, something we often find very hard in the West.

A visit to Diane's church was an indescribably moving experience, although I was grateful not to know ahead that it would last almost three hours. This Pentecostal church had a congregation of about 6,000 split between three services a day. Like many other Rwandans, Diane had not been prepared to return to the Catholic Church she felt had let them down so badly. The first hour of the service was devoted to praise led by a choir of over 100 singing in a mix of languages. There was so much emotion: tears, dancing, occasional whooping sounds and much joy. Over and over they would sing words like 'You are so full of grace, God, we thank you, and you bring peace, peace like a river, and if I have you I fear nothing'. I found it so hard to reconcile those passionately felt words with what had happened, but time and again we would see examples of what a Christian could understand to be God's redemption across this land and in its people. When I asked Diane whether she felt anger or bitterness, she spoke with a steely certainty.

'I can't forget what happened, of course I can't forget, but I want to move forwards, not go backwards. It is time for me to do my thing, to look for the future. I don't have time to waste on people, I mean bad people. I just don't have time for them, so if they exist or not, I don't care; I just want to focus on things that can help me and build my future. I don't really want to talk about what happened at all. I didn't when I was fourteen. It helps me to be with people who talk about something else and not those things. I think the only thing that can help you and heal you is prayers. People can come and talk to you and try to help but tomorrow they leave.

'When things happen to you, you just take it as it is. You can't do anything; you can't change anything. I think it depends on someone's personality, so for me I just realize that if I get mad or be angry or crying, it's not going to help anyway, so I just say let me do my life – if I don't, no one else is going to do it. I have some family, aunties and cousins, but I don't rely on them, if I tell the truth. Because I was an orphan when I was young, I had to be independent.

'If I think about my life now, I feel better. Now I can see something is happening in my life and I think God has helped. I really think God has helped me a lot to be where I am now, and what I did was not because I was stronger than anyone else, but God helped me to get where I am now. I went through all those things, things you can't explain to someone and you wonder why those things happened but you can't change it. That's why I told you I want to move on with my life – I don't even want to stay with people. I can't forget what my people went through but I want to help myself. When I was fourteen I didn't like someone who felt sorry for me; I wanted to make something of myself.'

As we ended our conversation, I knew that for Diane an epitaph would be a strange concept, but I asked her what she felt her most important characteristic was and if she had advice for others.

'I think I may say that I am strong and I have always had that spirit of being strong from my mother, but when I turned to Jesus, I got more strength. But what I may say is that every time there is time of trouble or time of happiness, I think what I may tell people is to try to accommodate every situation that happens to you. I know that God has a purpose for it because he knows what you are going through. What happened to me was God's purpose, otherwise I was going to die with everybody else.'

As Diane spoke with such forcefulness, I was struck by her determination and desire to achieve something. She could see the past only as holding her back. Although she has to focus on helping herself, she has often asked me to help other family members, and is always concerned for the friends she had made in Scotland. We had often joked about her wedding plans. She had told us about the importance of cows as a part of the celebrations, and we looked forward to the day we could take our Highland cows to Africa. A part of me longed to see her find a husband who would give her the love she deserved and would allow her to be herself and unburden her heart.

It was a privilege to know Diane, to visit Rwanda and to be given a glimpse of the circumstances of her suffering. It felt like the culmination of much that I had learned since Cameron died in 2001. I was beginning to understand the role of religious faith, to see the importance of prayer and of hope. Both Diane and Paula benefit from the strength and the structure that Christianity gives them. Although our world can be seen as shallow, I also heard Diane speak of the joy for her of coming to a place like Scotland where people smile and laugh – simple medicine for a wounded soul.

There is no doubt in my mind that I am blessed to know her, to consider her part of the family now. My family's relationship with her is a rare blessing for my children, too, and a gateway to their understanding of our troubled world and their need to respond in any way they can.

As our plane climbed into the African sky, heading for home, I thought of a biblical verse that our friend 'Uncle' John had written in a card for her as she left Scotland: 'Do not neglect to show hospitality to strangers, for by doing that some have entertained angels without knowing it' (Hebrews 13:2). As I read it I thought of Cameron, the angel in my life, and understood that the road I had chosen to take after her death had somehow led to Diane. Strangers cross our path every day of the week and we so rarely have time to meet them, but how many angels do we miss on the way?

9

OLIVIA GILES

Olivia Giles is a beautiful woman. This is one of the first things that people notice about her. She is also intelligent and charming and very lucky. At the age of thirty-six she had a turning point that very nearly took her life, when she became the victim of meningococcal septicaemia (the blood poisoning form of meningitis). She made a miraculous recovery but had to have her arms and legs amputated close to the knee and elbow joints, leaving her with no hands or feet.

I met Olivia at her house in Edinburgh. Dressed in black trousers and a black top, her wavy blond hair pulled back from her face, she looked slim and elegant. Her traditional stone house had a light-filled contemporary kitchen and a conservatory overlooking the garden. There were no obvious signs that life is not completely straightforward for her. It was only when she made a cappuccino and had to use a knife mounted on a short prosthetic arm to stir the milk that I was reminded of her disability. She manages to use her shortened arms to pick up a coffee mug and walks on her prosthetic legs with a barely discernible limp.

The moment I had first met Olivia over a year before, I sensed how alike we were, not only as the eldest of three sisters. We had both been determined career-driven women and had chosen to put our working lives first. I changed direction because of someone else's suffering. In Olivia's case, like Diane's, her new life had been forced upon her in terrifying circumstances. I am not sure that many people would have shown the courage she has in adapting to a very different life. She would prefer not to be some kind of 'poster girl' for the disabled, but there is no doubt that her story has inspired many people. I wanted to understand what it was that made her respond to her turning point in the way that she had.

'I'm the eldest of three girls, and I had a very lovely and secure childhood growing up in a small village outside Glasgow. My sisters are three and four years younger than me. I have always had all of the oldest child characteristics: responsible, worrier, diligent, conscientious. My dad was a quantity surveyor and mum was a primary school teacher. It was a typical Presbyterian, Church of Scotland outlook, and we regularly went to Sunday school or church until I was about sixteen. My parents worked hard to send us to private school because education was everything and it paid off for me.

'I think my work ethic, which is a big part of my character, came from my family. My parents are Conservative and had that view that if you work hard, everything will be all right and you will do well. But I also think that because of the security of my upbringing, I have a very natural optimism about life and it's quite hard to shake. I don't expect things to go wrong; I usually look for the good outcome, and it's only really in the latter years that I've realized that I do that and that it was shaped by my formative years.

'I started my education at an all girls' primary near my village and then was transferred to Hutchesons' Grammar School in Glasgow. I didn't enjoy secondary school one single bit; it was painful. I had friends, but I wasn't in the "in crowd", and I was definitely a bit of a misfit. I know it was because I was too immature for my year and I never really caught up. I worked hard and did well and left as soon as I could, but it did mean that I wound up in first-year law at Glasgow University at just seventeen, although at least I was staying at home. It was fine and it was a bit like a continuum of school, particularly doing law, which was fairly spoon-fed.

'After university, I came to Edinburgh to start my traineeship with Morton Fraser, which was a lovely cosy firm which suited me perfectly. Then I moved as a newly qualified lawyer to work in the commercial property department of Maclay, Murray and Spens, and my confidence really grew. I had been painfully shy as a child, but being able to do something well definitely made me a more confident person, whether being able to disagree with somebody or deal with difficult clients. As I got into my stride as a lawyer, I think I found my place in life. I was comfortable for the first time in my own skin – I was doing well; I had good prospects; I was enjoying it. I met my first husband when I joined the firm and was married to him within two years in 1991. After we separated in 1998, David told me that when I was made an associate in 1993, he'd thought, "That's great… Now maybe she'll take her foot off the gas and we'll start a family," but that his heart sank when I came home and said, "I've got that in the bag – now I'm going to be a partner." I can see now that we were actually just on different paths, but we have stayed good friends. At that stage, I believed in my heart that I wouldn't have been made a partner if I had children; I wasn't even thinking about it anyway. It was just a fact of life. Maclays is one of the best firms for equality, and I do think that I would have been supported, but I suppose I might have been frightened of my own ability to go back once I'd stopped. I really did see myself as a career woman and I was just achievement-driven from a very early age. You keep going, and if they raise the bar, you try harder, and the next "bar" was partnership and so I tried harder. I made partner at the age of thirty.

'If I look back at my character then, I was driven, determined and conscientious. I was a kind person, but my priorities were completely business-focused. It wasn't materialistic; I wasn't doing it for money. I was doing it to do a good job. I don't know who I was trying to impress. If it's there, you climb it and you do well. I didn't have time for family and friends. I found myself not even enjoying the "down time" that I was forced to have because my head was somewhere else. I mean I was there in body, but that was about it.

'If I think back to when I became ill, I had had a really heavy autumn – a horrible deal that really took it out of me – but I'd had a bit of a Christmas holiday and January had been OK. Around February, I could see work really starting to pick up again, but 21 February turned out to be the day I went to work for the last time. By teatime that day, I was just really unwell, and I don't normally get ill; I'm not an ill person. I was feeling a bit nauseous and felt like I must be getting the flu, except I didn't have any sniffles or a headache – I just felt rotten. It's hard to describe but I was so uncomfortable: I was absolutely freezing cold, and my hands and feet were like ice. I had my shoes off and my feet tucked up under me on my seat and I was getting nowhere with what was in front of me at work, but it was important and I thought I would be able to work through the night if I had to.

'Eventually I got my stuff together and got into the car to go home, realizing that I was not well. I staggered into the house, turned up the heating and got into bed. I had my coat and my winter boots on and I rolled myself up in the duvet and did at least get a bit warmer. I did get up at some point in the evening and changed into pyjamas and lots of socks and my dressing gown and got into bed with all that on.

'At that point, I was living with my partner, Robin, but he was out that night. In the morning, there was absolutely no way I could get out of bed, and Robin said I looked dreadful. The other thing which I only realized afterwards was that all through the night I had had a dreadful thirst and drank so much water, but I wasn't going to the loo. Robin called for a doctor, and there was an argument about whether I should go in to the surgery. I thought by that point that it was probably glandular fever because I didn't have any snivels. I didn't have a headache; I felt dreadful and my glands were swollen. I remember thinking, "I can't be ill. I can't be off work for months recovering."

'By now, I was starting to stiffen up, and by the time a doctor did actually come, after Robin called again, I had difficulty walking. I remember just sort of staggering along the hall and that my fingers couldn't really work on the door latch to let the doctor in, but she was really dismissive of me and my symptoms. I'm not blaming her for not diagnosing the disease, but she couldn't have been more unpleasant in her manner. I asked her to take a blood sample so they could actually test whether it was glandular fever – I sensed there was something major wrong with me. By now she was giving me the rolling eyes, and, strangely, that blood sample went missing, which would have confirmed what stage the disease was at. It was an awkward, awkward interview and she left having told me to stay in bed and take aspirin and that if I was really unhappy with what she was saying then I could always go to hospital. But the way she said it was as if "I'd obviously got a common virus and I'm making a fuss", so I thought I'll just get back in my box and be prepared to be off a day and I was thinking, "Gosh, if this is what a virus feels like... I'm so glad I've never had a virus before!" I went to sleep for a bit, and I still had all my work round me, which Robin had got from my briefcase. I had my mobile phone, and I was phoning the two girls that worked for me to check that they could do various things, and I was worrying that clients would think this was some made-up illness.

'The real sign that there was something very wrong was when I saw the splotches on my hands and feet. First of all I noticed them on my itchy feet when I peeled off the three pairs of socks to scratch them. There were these really big purple marks on them, and that was just off the scale of my experience. I immediately thought of our last holiday and wondered if I had some tropical disease, and then I looked at my hands and the backs were the same. If I'd known what the purple marks meant, I think I might have had a heart attack on the spot because I would have realized just how far-progressed the disease was. Even just for somebody to see something like that on their skin is bad enough – they almost seemed to be growing as I was looking at them.

'I lay there for a good ten minutes thinking, "She said I had a virus. I was to stay in bed. Don't be a hypochondriac – don't make a fuss; think it through" and, on the other hand, feeling blind panic. Eventually, I worked it through and thought, "OK, I don't care if she thinks I'm stupid – I'm going to hospital!" I phoned the surgery and I asked for the doctor, and I said, "Before you say anything, get me an ambulance – get it now, and I'm not taking any argument!" Unbelievably, she asked me, "Could you not drive yourself?" and I screamed, I really screamed at her because I was so frightened by that time.

'The whole ambulance procedure was horrible. I saw the ambulance shape outside my house, but although my mind was fine my body wasn't working properly. I started thinking about things like clean knickers if I was going to be in hospital overnight, but I actually couldn't really move properly to get things together. I put my coat on over my dressing gown and tried to find my handbag, and I just got to the door as he was about to drive away. Fortunately, he saw me and he came running up the path, took one look at me and carried me to the ambulance. He put me in it, got me an oxygen mask, bundled me up in blankets, and at that point I was starting to think, "This wasn't in my game plan for today." He was swearing about the situation to the ambulance service because he'd been sent as a single crew, but he couldn't drive me because I was too ill to be left in the back on my own. So we then had to sit there and wait while an ambulance with a double crew came. I remember being in A & E, and I remember thinking, "Surely it can't be as bad as an emergency...?" But I did get a real sense of panic because there was such a commotion going on, and I heard the word "meningitis" and I heard "toxic shock", and then Robin arrived at the hospital. I really don't have a good sense of the timescale, but Robin arrived and they may just have put me "under" at that point, but it seemed to me that when he came, I could stop, I could just let go. I knew nothing more for the next four to five weeks.

'That night, they sent Robin home, and they said that I was probably going to die and there wasn't really anything they could do. They would need to be dealing with me all the time and they would call. So the fact that I made it through that night was a good thing. After about two weeks, they'd stabilized the infection, so they were looking then at how far the gangrene was going to spread. It had come up right over my elbows and knees; my shoulders were black and it was showing on my face. They thought they were going to have to amputate above the elbow and above the knee on both sides. My parents and Robin were told, "Do you want this, because it doesn't have to be that way... we could let her go..."

'I think everybody – my sisters, my best friend, David my ex-husband – they were all in the overnight pow-wow about what to do. Robin has told me quite recently that they went into the hospital the next day intending to say goodbye but not quite believing it. My mum said that she didn't actually decide; she just prayed that something would change. And something did change because the surgeon, Mr Awf Quaba, had been brought in to look at the x-rays, and he reckoned that he had a chance of being able to save the joints with skin-grafting. Although he couldn't guarantee success, he said he would tackle each joint one at a time, and, in fact, the decision was taken away from everyone because there was a chance of saving some of my knees and elbows, so nobody ever actually had to say what they would do.

'If you think about it from Robin's point of view, if it had been an above-elbow, above-knee amputation, he would have been left with a completely dependent torso... for life! Well, I wasn't married to him then, but for him that must have been a pretty horrific prospect too.

'Looking back, there was no single moment when I woke and understood what had happened to me. It was a really gradual realization. I do remember being told that the reason I couldn't hold a cup was because I had no hands and thinking, "Don't be so ridiculous... they're inside the bandages!" I've thought about this a lot, and I think that it's a self-protection mechanism. I think that I knew, but until I could cope with it, I didn't really let the information filter through. There was no one moment where somebody said, "This is the story..." It wasn't like that. I was drugged up, and I would say it was at least a fortnight after I was conscious before I actually knew and could say to you, "Yes, my hands and feet have been amputated," and by that time I was coping. I didn't let it touch me until I'd got my coping strategy in place.

'My strategy was very much about, "What's happening right now? Can I cope with right now? Can I cope with the next hour?" That was it... one step at a time. The whole rehabilitation period was amazing, it was so rewarding and joyful. It was like getting a chance to be born again and to learn to do everything again so it was like getting all the joy of being a child but accelerated into a few months. It was all forward-looking. There were a few dreadful days in hospital. I remember getting blisters after I got my prosthetic legs and not being able to get up on them for days. I'm not saying it was a picnic – it was really hard work, but I like hard work. I didn't know what was going to happen, but I didn't have any major setbacks along the way. The general trend was up. It was not like having a degenerative disease. It was not like getting a horrible diagnosis. I got a second chance and that was how it felt.

'I had no depression at all, and I put it down to the way I was handled by the incredible nurses at St John's in Livingstone, where I had the surgery and the real psychological processing was happening. The personal bit of nursing is just as important as the hands-on stuff. If I'd got the message "Disaster! Look at you – you're broken, you're mutilated, you look dreadful, you might never walk again...," maybe I would've been depressed, but I didn't ever get that message. The message I got was "Do you know how lucky you are to be alive?" I understood very early on that it was an absolute bloody miracle that I was actually breathing and I had my elbows and my knees.

'I really did focus on what I had, rather than on what I'd lost, but it's much easier to do that when you have got so much. I have a loving family; I have a great husband (Robin and I got married later); I have great sisters and friends; so I wasn't some poor soul on my own. I think the care everyone gave me is part of who I am now because it was just so built in to how I tackled things and what I thought about myself and what I was worth.

'I think that my story catches people's attention because losing limbs is a big deal in people's minds, but sometimes the bigger deals are easier to deal with because you have people's sympathy. Only three people have ever said anything heartless to me: three men who made it so obvious that they found how I look now repellent. It hurt because it made me realize that what I looked like was all they ever really liked about me before.

'I'm lucky that Robin never made me feel any different at all. It never crossed my mind to be embarrassed or to think that he would leave me. I'm sure he must have had his moments, but I don't think we are together because of what I look like. He never related to me in a different way. He has been absolutely constant, as hard on me and as demanding and as rude and cheeky as he always was, right from the beginning. He makes jokes all the time about me. If we are in a shop and I'm taking too long, he'll say, "Oh well, at least we can skip past the nail polish!" He is just ordinary with me and always was.

'I can do most of what I need to do to live my life. I can't do housework but I don't have to. I get frustrated with paperwork and cooking, standing can get sore after half an hour, and I can only carry one thing at a time so setting a table is a drag, but at least I can do it even if it's slow. I can drive, which gives me independence.

'Some people do have a problem with me not wearing prosthetic hands, but I think once people actually know you and they're talking to you as a person, they just forget. It doesn't seem an issue to me. Occasionally I'll get noticed by some kids who say, "Mummy, mummy... look, that lady's got no hands!" and mummy looks like she wants to melt into the floor with embarrassment. But most of the time I forget that I look different. I'm more frustrated with what I can't do than with what I look like. I do want my hair to be nice and I wouldn't go out without make-up, but I just think that's a case of putting your best foot forward. I'm less bothered about clothes than I was; I just want to look presentable and not draw attention to myself. I don't think that my idea of self-worth was ever particularly tied to what I looked like. My mother never led me to believe that I was anything special to look at. I think that by the time that I turned thirty, I realized that I could hold my own in a crowd looks-wise, no more than that, but it was not until then that I actually thought maybe I could use this. But I never thought it was important. There are other things that you could take away that I would value more. I can't imagine not being able to talk or see. I don't think that what's happened to me is a disaster because of how much I've got left, but I know it's not the same for everybody.

'I did have questions and I wanted to understand what had happened and why it had happened. I was angry for quite a long time with the locum who hadn't picked up meningitis because it's a human reaction to want to blame misfortune on some thing, but I will never know whether, if she'd come earlier or if she'd sent me straight to hospital, it would have made any difference. I realized once I met her again that she was just somebody who had made a mistake, like I've made plenty of mistakes. I think that with absolutely everything, if you can't change it you have to accept that it is the way it is. That's probably the kindest thing you can do for yourself rather than trying to say, "I wish it hadn't happened" or "I wish it was different…".

'I don't know if this turning point for me has made me a better person, but I think that when you go through something tough yourself you become so much more aware of other people's issues and suffering. I think that one thing I do which is different now is that if I am spending time with somebody, I will really engage with them – I will try to understand where they're coming from as a person, and I won't just sit and pass the time thinking about what is on my desk. It is a bit of a gift to get a pause like that in the middle of your life – at thirty-six to be forced to stop and do nothing. I had been getting on with life, but I did realize that I was on a hamster wheel. I realized that I was living to work rather than working to live, and I did not know how to break that cycle. I would not have broken that cycle on my own. I needed to be ejected, and I do wonder who or what pressed the button. Was it my own will or a benign God of some kind?

'I wouldn't use the word "happy" to describe myself because it's a bit too light and frivolous, but I'm definitely much, much more content with my lot now than I was, and I just think I've developed so many more resources to be able to cope with what life throws at you. The reason is that I have a deeper appreciation and understanding of what it means to be alive and what your potential is when you're here and that you haven't got a huge amount of time to mess about. I'm really sorry that I don't have children, and it's not likely to happen, but you can focus a lot on what you haven't got, and nobody has an entitlement to their wish list.

'I lost a lot of my identity when I lost my career, and that has always been very difficult to come to terms with. I miss the intellectual challenge and the badge of achievement that goes with being a professional. I'm very, very achievement-driven, and having worked my whole life to get that badge, it was very hard to take it off. Nowadays I am still very busy, but I am glad not to be on the same conveyor belt I was on since about the age of five and that I have a chance to choose, to lift my head and look around at what else is possible. What I had been doing with my life was making rich people richer, and I have a different sense of what is important now. I would like to feel when I got to seventy-two that I had made more of a contribution. I do think that if you get an opportunity in life, you've got an obligation to deliver on it. That sense of obligation comes from my upbringing. I think it would be awful to think that you'd wasted a second chance; that would be worse than wasting the first chance.

'My work for charity started slowly, with people asking me to do things. When you've been lying in hospital, it feels really empowering to be able to do *anything*. For quite a long time, I spoke at just about anything, and I turned up at just about anything. Then I thought I could do something of my own for the meningitis cause, and that became a nine-month plan leading up to an event in February 2004 called "Leap for Meningitis", which raised £485,000. It was really empowering to realize that I was able to do something that was different.

'The awards I have been given, such as my honorary degrees, are very nice, but I struggle with getting an award for what seems to be simply getting up and living my life. I feel a bit of a fraud. Perhaps the awards are for doing something which I don't have to? I suppose I could just have a nice life – go to the cinema and go out to lunch. But at the end of the day, I'm not doing what I do for anybody but myself. We all do what we're doing for ourselves, so that we can live up to our expectations of ourselves. I still expect to work hard and to do well, but the direction of my effort is different. I don't think your deep-rooted drivers and character ever change, but you can choose to point them in a different direction. For me, achievement is not about having your name in lights. It can be very private. Nobody needs to know what you have done, as long as you know that you did everything you could to the best of your ability. That is what counts, but I have changed the emphasis and my priorities. For example, I now make more time for my family and to meet friends and for holidays and my marriage.

'Looking back, religion has played a part in my life. I had a childlike, innocent fervour as a child, and I actually knew the Bible quite well. I knew the arguments for the difficult Christian questions at really quite a young age. I suppose that as my thinking became a little more critical in secondary school, I started to doubt that every word of the Bible was true and to try to figure out where other religions fitted in. And that left me feeling guilty over not being able to just have blind faith in Christianity.

'My minister for my communicants class, Johnston Mackay, was an interesting thinker. He was bold enough to admit that he did have doubts, and I found that liberating. I felt that maybe it was OK not to know all the answers and to pick and choose the parts of religions that mean something to you and inspire you to be the best you can be. For example, I loved his forensic examination of the Easter story, which seemed to prove that it all happened as a historical event. I love the hope that brings – but I don't think that means I also have to believe that Jesus is the only route to God. What about all the people brought up as Muslims or with no faith at all?

'I think all the religions are just different people's interpretations of something so massive and so far beyond our comprehension that we can't possibly get our heads round it. All religions seem to argue that their representative of God on earth is the only legitimate one. I am not arguing with Christianity as a way of life; there's nothing to pick holes in with "love thy neighbour". I just struggle with the idea that Jesus is the only way to God. I have a problem with organized religion which is so rigid, dogmatic, intolerant and arrogant as not to recognize the other ones or another way.

'I think we've all got a capacity for spirituality and to be in touch with something beyond this life on earth. As a result of what I've been through, I'm far more convinced than I was before that there is something else, a grand plan, a higher intelligence, because I think that the miracle of life is too incredible for it to be just an accident. For me the clues are the way some things just come together apparently supernaturally: the moments when you feel an overwhelming compassion for humanity as if we are all part of the same whole and occasionally meeting people that you just know are "old souls". I suppose it's just a heightened awareness of what it means to be alive.

'I didn't rely on prayer to get me through what happened, but my residual faith was and is a comfort for me, because I need to know that there's more than this. I would find it very hard to think that you die and that's it. Letting myself off the hook of having to have it all worked out has brought me a lot of peace of mind. I probably did get a lot from other people, from the humanity of the people around me. For me I feel that it wasn't quite my time – I definitely held on for something, and that might be part of my sense of obligation.

'If I think about an epitaph, what others might say and what I would want them to say are probably worlds apart. My ex-husband and probably Robin would say, "She worked very hard," and I wouldn't want that. I would probably want, "She made a difference." I'd like to have left things better than I found them. I'd like to have touched people.'

Olivia's life has already touched many people in so many ways, and it is typical of her that she would think she might not be remembered for that. She has a remarkable humility, which perhaps stems from her lack of confidence as a child. She doesn't feel that she deserves the awards she has received, but there is no doubt that she has been a high achiever in her new life. Her 'Leap for Meningitis' event raised a staggering amount of money, and her honorary degrees were not only for her 'personal courage' but also for her work as a trained mediator for the NHS and for her key role in advising the government on health and social care policy, particularly in relation to rehabilitation. The charity 500 Miles, which she co-founded, is developing a prosthetics centre in Malawi that involves many challenges, including some difficult travelling – yet another example of Olivia constantly raising the bar.

Olivia's turning point has resulted in a new life that most of us could not begin to imagine. The psychological impact of being told that she was a miracle was significant to her and is something she continues to talk about to remind those in the caring professions of its importance. It is remarkable that she can describe her rehabilitation as a joyful experience. Her beauty, which of course is partly physical but comes also from character, is one of the first things you notice about her, and it means that when some people meet her, their first thought is not one of pity. But above all her courage, her determination to be in control and her positive attitude – the very characteristics that defined her in her career – were and are essential keys and tools for her recovery and for her future. Olivia's story shows a tremendous determination and ability to accept things that she cannot change – not unlike Diane's. And yet, like Diane, she simply refuses to allow circumstances to take over her life; she is determined to move on.

10

CHRIS MOON

Chris Moon is another example of an individual who has been determined not to let major setbacks ruin his life. I was intrigued by the story of a man who has had more than his share of disasters, from his kidnapping by the Khmer Rouge to an amputated arm and leg at the age of thirty-three, as a result of a landmine accident in Mozambique. In both cases, he survived against all the odds. These were major turning points in his life, and he had a choice to become a victim of these circumstances or to decide to make something of them. He chose the latter route, founding a successful motivational speaking business and constantly challenging himself physically, running marathons all over the world in extreme conditions such as the 250-kilometre Great Sahara Run, known as the toughest footrace on earth. He has won numerous awards and medals for his work for charity.

I met Chris on a wintry morning at a hotel outside Edinburgh, not far from the Scottish home he shares with his wife Alison and three boys. I had read many articles about him and wondered as I waited whether I would warm to someone who seemed so confident and tough. In interviews, he appeared to reflect the British 'stiff upper lip' approach, and yet I was intrigued by what was so often left unsaid. Thankfully, Chris was an easy interviewee: charming, articulate and humorous once he started to relax. Dressed in a typical country outfit of checked shirt and tweed jacket, his disabilities were not apparent when we first met, except when we shook hands. His response was to put his left hand forward to shake rather than offering you the mechanized hook which forms the end of his prosthetic right arm – a natural move for him which helps put you at ease. His prosthetic leg gives him a slight limp, and it was only when coming down the stairs without a banister on his right side that I became aware of any nervousness, but more on my part than his.

He spoke with tremendous passion and conviction, keenly interested in my own situation and asking many questions about my recent trip to Bosnia. He seemed curious about my opinion on a variety of subjects and was warm in his congratulations on the work of ProjectScotland. Eventually he began to tell me about the years that led up to his kidnapping and referred to the influence of religion in his life.

'I grew up with my sister and two cats in a stone farmhouse in a small village in Wiltshire. My dad worked for a company supplying agricultural seeds and fertilizers, and my mum ran the Girl Guides and worked as a secretary and accounts clerk. They were kind people, helping others out whenever they could. It was a happy world of summer fetes and holidays on my uncle's farm, and I went to a nearby grammar school. Church on Sunday was a big part of my life. I don't think that I have much interest in religion, but I realize now that my childhood was quite influenced by the church and the concept of right and wrong as a code for living. We all need rules, even a simple philosophy of tolerance and kindness and one in which we won't do something to somebody else that we wouldn't want done to us. It just seems a very good way to live as people, but clearly some people are violent and destructive and negative and you've got to be strong enough to stand up to it. Religion for some people gives an element of certainty and saves them thinking, whereas my own philosophy of life would be much more about thinking and understanding, learning about our own emotions and other people's motives. It is about a search for the truth. I find meaning in taking control of my destiny, finding a reason for living and doing what I think is the right thing to do.

'After school I went to agricultural college but soon realized that this wasn't the smartest business to be in economically, although a lovely way of life. I began at that point to ask what I really wanted out of life. I wanted to do something humanitarian and service-orientated so I decided to join the army. At that time, the infantry was taking a preventative role, so I chose to be an officer in the Royal Military Police. Holding people accountable in war seemed a right and proper and decent thing to do, and I believe in the rule of law – laws are the cement that holds societies together. I think most people want to feel they're doing something worthwhile and they're making a contribution, and many of the people I speak to in the corporate world want to do something that makes a difference; it's a human desire. The truth is, if we can do something that will add value and meaning to someone's life or will help somebody, it will add value and meaning to our own existence.'

Yet again, I was hearing words that made sense to me and many of those I was interviewing. However, his life in the army may not have fulfilled such aspirations. He clearly enjoyed his three years on the operational side but knew the army was under pressure as 'options for change' evolved, and he decided to leave. He had a brief foray into the financial world but still felt, at the age of thirty-one, that he wanted something more. I was surprised that he should then choose to do something as dangerous as volunteering to clear landmines in Cambodia for the charity Halo Trust, made famous by the interest of Diana, Princess of Wales. I would have thought that most men at his age would be more concerned about job security and starting a family. Much as he might play down the risks, he was soon the victim of a kidnapping by the Khmer Rouge and became one of the few Westerners to survive this, having managed to negotiate their release and then walk overnight for 50 kilometres through a patrolled and mined jungle.

'I was determined to do something where I felt I was actively making a contribution to humanity, living my spiritual ideals, so I chose to go and work for a charity. I always knew I could come back and earn a living, so I wasn't particularly worried about the long term. I also don't think it is that dangerous. Having said that, I know seven people who are now dead but mostly because of the environments they were in. I know I was lucky to survive a kidnapping by men who were genocidal maniacs. They ambushed our vehicles and forced me and my Cambodian colleagues to drive miles through the remote jungle to their camp. The locals assumed we would have been dead within twenty-four hours.

'I realize now how fortunate we were, because I went back and made a documentary for Channel 4 and Discovery, and I met the Khmer Rouge commander who made the decision not to execute us. I had no idea that it was pretty much a done deal, and he was there to rubber stamp it. Put yourself in their position: you have no natural education, no parenting relationship; you base your information on the outside world, on what you hear on Khmer Rouge radio, which never won any awards for impartial reporting. Because we had a Russian truck they said we were Cambodian government, and I was a military adviser and they kept asking if I was Russian. It would have been an extraordinary kind of injustice if I had died.'

It is typical of Chris's style in his autobiography to describe his kidnapping as 'having a bad day', and he even tries to suggest that there were positives. While I am thinking ahead to the outcomes of this key turning point in his life, in his typical humorous fashion he lowers the tone a bit by commenting that 'We weren't buggered – that was a big positive... That was a very big positive, as far as I was concerned. You always

think it could happen when you're a prisoner, don't you...
It's one of those thoughts.' Although quick to make light of
the situation, I knew he must have felt real fear, particularly as
on about seven occasions they overheard their captors talking
about shooting them. He describes an incident shortly after
they were captured.

'We were suddenly told to take our clothes off, and we were
surrounded by thick thorn trees so you couldn't run through
them, and I actually started to think, "Oh God, something's
happened, something's changed. They want to keep our clothes;
they're just going to shoot us." And had anyone done anything
stupid and ran away they probably would've been shot, so it was
all about keeping calm, and then I began to say, "Right, well,
maybe something has changed. If it has, and they are just going
to gun us down here, there's not going to be a lot I can do. I
can't run through these trees, so start looking for a strategy."
I couldn't come up with any answers; I was responsible for
my people, and I couldn't come up with any answers. I take
leadership extremely seriously. I take responsibility very
seriously, and I was responsible for all these people and yet
there was nothing I could do.

'I felt awful, and then I looked down the line and I saw the
de-miner on the end of the line being told to take his watch off
to give to the soldier, and I thought, "Right, no matter what
happens, I will never assume the role of victim." I know from
my military training that when you're a prisoner you lose all
concept of time, so I tucked my watch down the back of my
underpants, and I think the soldiers thought I was just very
afraid as I shuffled forward to the Land Rover with a bulge in
the back of my underpants.

'I believe that the eyes are the window of the soul, and you
could look in those soldiers' eyes and think they were just
dead. There was no spark; there was nothing – no kindness,
no interaction – they just had dead, brutal eyes. I realized at

that moment there would be no point in asking for mercy or compassion because they couldn't feel it. It was such a powerful, lonely experience, because I was on my own, and it's when I learned to be totally self-reliant and not be a victim. I think that's the best survival strategy. I decided I would strive to compel my circumstances, not to be compelled by circumstance, and that's the battle we face in life: to compel our circumstances, not to be compelled by circumstance.

'I was really frightened, but the interesting thing is that when you are literally in fear of your life, you get to the stage where you only have so much capacity to feel it and you become resigned to your fate and get used to anything. You do get this feeling of dread, but remember we only have so much capacity to feel these things. People talk a lot about the survival mechanism, but there's one mechanism that's much more powerful than that and that's the death mechanism. We start to become resigned to our fate, and if you look at how people react, it's the three "f's": fight, fright or flight.

'I believe the human spirit has the ability to rise above most things, and we can tolerate almost anything if we have reasons more important than ourselves to do so. Then again, I did pray – every time I thought we were going to be killed, I prayed that we might somehow be able to influence the circumstances, and I think that there is the power of good, God, love, creativity, kindness. I find this hard, but this experience has made me less dogmatic; it has made me realize that frequently religious people are very judgmental, and my concept of God is that it isn't about being judgmental. I admit that I have experienced times where things happen that are just more than coincidence.

'I remember many years before that I woke up in the middle of the night, and I had just had this really very bizarre experience in a dream, and after that I couldn't go back to sleep. I had this feeling of motion, like I was floating. It was a really weird experience and it was incredibly hot. Then I could smell this beautiful perfume, and I looked out the window and I could see these trees lying and leaves on the ground and a tree trunk. And then suddenly everything was dark and I had this feeling of falling, and then it was beautifully cool and I had this feeling of rising. I saw this vivid yellow, vivid blue and then a fluttering, you know, of yellow and blue butterflies. And it was so weird, such a bizarre experience, because I actually felt the heat of that moment and then the coolness, the falling, the rising… and I just didn't go back to sleep.

'I'm reluctant normally to talk about this because it's very difficult if people haven't experienced this; it's like trying to describe colours to a blind person. There'll be people who will be very sceptical of this, and they just won't be able to get their head round it, but I even went back and found the spot later. When I got to Cambodia, I had that dream again; I remember it very clearly, and I couldn't go back to sleep. I remember it because it was such an extreme experience, and then, when I was in the jungle, it happened again. As we were being forced to drive over bumpy tracks in the Land Rover, there was an overpowering scent of perfume, which turned out to be sandalwood. The heat was gone and it was wonderfully cool. We were surrounded by an incredibly beautiful mass of yellow and blue butterflies, just as I had seen in my dream. It gave me an immense feeling of reassurance. I somehow felt that it was divine providence, God's will, that I was meant to be there. It gave me a definite sense of purpose, and although I didn't know that I was going to live, I knew that whatever happened, it was meant to be and that I was in the right place at the right time. I also became even more determined to compel circumstance rather than be compelled.

'I had the most bizarre experience with the Khmer Rouge commander the next day when I met him. As I looked around me and saw those dead eyes, I started to think, "This looks really bad." We were in their territory and they were in no hurry to do anything or go anywhere, and they wouldn't take us into any of the villages as they didn't want anybody to know that I was there, which was scary. I said, "Look, God, please help me, just give me the chance of communicating with someone who can understand this," because, you realize, these guys thought I was their enemy, and I'd listened to everything they'd said and they were accusing me of being a foreign military adviser. I realized if we broke the rules we'd be killed, and they had absolute authority to do it. Then, when I met the commander, the first thing he said was "Ah, there was a voice in my head this morning which told me I had to stay here, as there would be something very important to do this afternoon, and you're that reason," and he then made the decision for us not to be executed.

'I met the commander some years later for the documentary and wondered what he had meant by "that reason". I hadn't realized that, as a result of having made the decision not to execute us, his own execution was ordered by Pol Pot. He got wind of it and ended up having to defect, which worked out very well for him in the end. When I asked him, he said he was really proud of his time in the Khmer Rouge, but the thing he didn't like was having to kill too many people. He wasn't a butcher and a murderer in the sense of the "Killing Fields"; it was the militias that did all of that. He was a soldier, and I could find some nobility in him – he was a warrior. I'm not saying that he was a good man, but I'm saying there was good in him and he was able to see the bigger picture, which was what I had prayed for – somebody who had the capacity to understand – and by building a relationship with him, I survived. When I asked him the question about my survival, he just said, "I decided you were a good person and you weren't afraid." There was something in me that he could see in himself, and it was about finding the common ground. Since then, I've always striven to be a good person and to look for decency and goodness in others. I also realized I should be more confident having been able to live through that experience.'

The incident in Cambodia had clearly been a major turning point in Chris's life. His survival seemed to me to be almost miraculous, and perhaps that explains why he chose not to take an easy path next. He refused to take any leave after the experience and continued to work in Cambodia for a while before being transferred to Mozambique to continue clearing landmines. It was here that he would suffer his next traumatic and most life-changing experience as a result of being blown up by a landmine. It had been left in an area that had supposedly been cleared, and Chris described what it felt like to be blown up.

'It's f***ing loud. The loudest thing you can imagine – to feel the blast and to hear the noise of the explosion at the same time – that's my overwhelming memory of it all. It was really loud, and then it was really peaceful. My mind raced, and I thought that I was in Cambodia and I'd been hit by a mortar. Then I looked at the grass and realized it was African grass and realized in that split second there was only one possible explanation for the blast. I remember it very clearly as if it was a few minutes ago; it's a very extreme feeling. As I looked down, I saw there was a hole in the back of my right hand – the same size as the de-mining tool that I'd been holding. I realized that the worst thing that can happen is that both legs will be blown off, my guts will be hanging out, and I'll be about to die, and I thought, "OK, accept the fact that you may well have lost limbs; I've gotta face it, whatever it is." So I forced myself to look down, and I see my lower left leg is still there. It's a bit burned, but my lower right leg has been completely blown off and was in little bits everywhere, but already it's not as bad as it could be if I had lost both legs. I was quite curious that the bone was yellow when I had expected it to be white. I shout my medical status back to the team on the road – that's the drill – and then I start thinking that I'm going to be very, very fortunate to get out of this alive; I'm a long way from anywhere. I start thinking, "Right, gotta make the best of it." So, I was there on my own for a bit until the back-up team came, and I thought about what had happened just before the blast. I was walking through this clear lane, and I thought, "Something is not quite right." I remember the feeling very clearly, that something vile and evil was coming towards me. I felt a rising sense of panic as I turned to get away from it. I took three paces and... Bang!

'They say the body produces endorphins so you feel no pain for the first few minutes – absolutely true – then after that it's a bit sore. The first thing that hurt was my left foot; my sock had melted to my ankle, and I laughed, because here I was with a leg completely blown off and a badly damaged right hand but that was what hurt most. I remember it very clearly, and then the pain just got worse and worse and worse, and there seemed to be no ceiling to the pain. I kept thinking, "This pain can't get any worse, this pain can't get any worse, this pain can't get any worse," then a couple of hours later in hospital in the nearby town I remember thinking, "Hmmm... maybe it just keeps on getting worse." It reaches a point at which you would rather be dead, but I think for me dying was the easy option. There is a death mechanism, a feeling that death's not that bad – just fade out, go to sleep. But I couldn't do that because I thought of all the times that I'd not necessarily made the best of life, so I decided that even if I only had a few more breaths left, I was going to fight for every breath that I had and not give up. I said my prayers and said, "Look, God, forgive me for the bad things that I've done; haven't got time to mention them all...," and then I wished I'd done a few more bad things, and then I thought, "Right – fight for life, God help me." All I got was another wave of pain, but maybe it was the pain that kept me alive.

'Somehow I managed to keep control and get my body armour off as the medics arrived. I was put in a helicopter and stabilized. But I began to feel that I was dying from not enough fluid. I had this terrible burning in my throat, and the medic was struggling to get the drip into me. I decided that rather than be compelled by circumstances, I would use my imagination, and I just decided that it would be sensible to grab hold of the blood replacement solution and drink it. I thought it was the last thing I was going to do, and if I didn't do it I wouldn't be around, so I just thought intelligently. It's really quite amusing, because all these people afterwards were saying that a casualty shouldn't drink, but I lived, so what does it matter what people think? I realize that we live in a world of hindsight heroes, with people who talk about events at which they weren't present and put their own interpretation on it. That's one thing being blown up taught me.

'When I eventually got to the hospital in Johannesburg, I just wasn't bothered that I'd lost a leg and hand. I'd lived. I was very pleased to be alive. I had six major operations and stayed there for almost a month. When I came back to London to a rehabilitation hospital, it was no different. I got a taxi back, went straight into hospital and thought, "Right, recovery plan," and saw my family that afternoon, no problem at all. I asked them not to get too upset about things, and they didn't. My mum was very good; she didn't blub. I was very pleased to be alive, but I just wanted to get on with life and make the best of it.

'I had made a decision to clear landmines. I never thought I'd be injured, as it's very unusual, but it happened, and there are some things in life that you have to accept with good grace and this is one of them. If our true focus is being involved with others and we are not the centre of our own universe, then automatically what happens to us will not be the be-all and end all-of our existence. Some people I've seen, sadly, have really struggled with disability, have been in positions where their main focus in life is themselves, and then of course that makes it very difficult. I know it sounds strange, but I got my head round it all straight away.

'Friends came to take me out from hospital, but I wasn't going to do the victim bit. We just had a great laugh, and the fact that I'd lost a couple of bits of my body was really irrelevant: we were all still the same people, and we were able to laugh at the funny bits of adapting to new circumstances. People were very supportive and kind. I already understood the importance of willpower and the importance of imagination – the importance of having a centre of focus that was beyond the end of your own nose – and I understood that sometimes in life you've got to take the pain and be resilient and keep on getting up every time you fall over. So I knew all that, which was a good position to start from, facing some of the challenges that I'd chosen to face. From my kidnapping I thought, "Well, if I can cope with that, I can cope with this," so I had an attitude in which I knew I would always find a way to cope.

'I don't bother with people who are negative, and I've decided not to do negative issues. It's like bitterness; think of someone you know who has suffered an injustice: are they fun to be with? Nobody wants to be near a bitter person, so I spend time with positive people, and I'm not saying I don't try and help people, especially if friends are having a tough time, but I try and put a positive perspective on it. Some people revel in negativity, in negative criticism of others, even those trying to make a difference. I've focused on what I have, not what I've lost.

'I have had a lot of involvement in charity work, but I also have my business as a motivational speaker called Making the Best, as I have a family to provide for. I am the proof that what I say works. I know how to cope, and the difference between me now and ten years ago is that firstly I have no ego; I'm just very grateful to be alive, so I don't have any points to prove. When I'm doing a presentation, it's not about me; it's about the experiences that I've learned and what relevance they can have to people. I talk about many different things: mindset, motivation and leadership. What we need to recognize is that we need to give ourselves a positive pep talk, and we need to be positive and tell ourselves that we can do it. Tell ourselves to get up and keep on getting up. People must believe in themselves, and most people can deal with an awful lot more than they think if they choose to believe they can. Success for me is knowing that I've impacted on some people positively.

'Nowadays, I'm very much a lover of the natural world. I find great peace in my garden; I feel very close to God there. Also, achieving goals and helping someone to do something they didn't necessarily believe they could do – that really gives me a buzz. I'm not sure that I would write an epitaph for myself, but I suppose if I had to, it would be that I took responsibility, made the best of life and loved life, but do you know what you think of when you're dying? All you want is a bit of love, someone to hold your hand. That's what you think of when you're dying; you just want a human touch. And that's probably the truth of life – it's about loving and being loved.

'If I was to summarize what these two key turning points and all my experiences have taught me, it is to take responsibility for who you are and where you are, work out where you want to be, dream, set goals, but have some idea of a destination and work out how you're going to get there, what it is you want to achieve. Remember that life is all about people: it's about loving and being loved; it's about making the best of life and connecting with like-minded people, about forming relationships with people who will support you on your journey, who will understand why you wanted to get there and recognize also that it's give and take, that the nature of relationships is that they should be about interdependence. And, once on our journey, we need to realize the importance of persistence: it's about getting up every time you fall over and keeping on getting up.

'A key moment in my life was making that choice to go and work for Halo, to control my destiny, to make a choice to say, "Right, where do I want to go? What do I want to do?" Once I'd made that choice to do something worthwhile, to make a contribution and to take total responsibility for myself, even though some pretty challenging things have happened, I've never regretted it. You have to go to the furthest point if you want to get to the grace of God.'

By the end of our conversation, it was clear that Chris had an extraordinary ability to articulate thoughts and ideas that many often found very hard to explain. The challenges he had faced seemed to give him a right to push people to make the best of themselves and not to be a victim of circumstances. So often in my work I would meet people who felt that it was impossible for them to rise above their own difficult situation. I remember spending a week at Columba 1400 on Skye with a wonderful group of young people who felt trapped by the tough area that they grew up in, finding it hard to imagine an escape, particularly when outsiders can be so quick to be judgmental about them.

His story of cheating death twice is remarkable and inspirational, although I still wonder how many others could find the reserves of courage and strength to get through something similar. Once again, upbringing and family values were important, and he recognizes the importance of his own forward-looking attitude and that of the positive people around him who give him support. It seems hard to believe that what happened has not cost him dearly in some ways, but it seems his suffering had a purpose, and he has been able to demonstrate that in everything he has done since these turning points in his life. Making a difference to others can be a way of helping deal with your own problems. I was glad that he was prepared to tell me the story of the butterflies and to let me see beyond the confident action man to the emotions that run deep.

Chris mentioned a quote by Theodore Roosevelt that is meaningful to him: 'It is not the critic who counts; not the man who points out how the strong man stumbles or where the doer of deeds could have done better. The credit belongs to the man who is actually in the arena... You've never lived until you've almost died. For those who have had to fight for it life has truly a flavour the protected shall never know.'

11

SEAN CORRIGAN

Many of the individuals in this book have suffered in various ways, whether because of a tragic loss, injury or a dramatic illness. In most cases, they took these various challenges in their stride and continued to move forward. In Sean Corrigan's story, there was no particular turning point in his life that made him into a drug addict, but he did need a turning point for him to recover. Sean had reached the end of all his resources when he arrived in the village of Medjugorje in June 2000 to join the Cenacolo Community. Our paths would cross during my first visit there in April 2001, and he was to have a remarkable impact on me as part of my own turning point.

Medjugorje is a village in Bosnia, a place of pilgrimage for many Christians. In 1981, the first reports reached Britain that the Virgin Mary was appearing to a group of local children, and these apparitions continue today. Millions of people have now visited the village, and a number of charitable projects have sprung up in the area. The Cenacolo Community is one of them, a Christian association with over fifty communities across the world. Founded in 1983 by an Italian nun, Sister Elvira Petrozzi, its mission is to help drug addicts and lost youth with a simple life of work, friendship and prayer.

I can remember very clearly my first visit to Cenacolo. We had climbed a steep road out of the village and passed through iron gates into a peaceful oasis with attractive brick buildings surrounded by well-tended flowerbeds. We were directed towards a tiny chapel; our group of twelve entered through a low door and sat on simple stone bench seats around the walls. A shaft of light filtered through the window by the altar, adding to the sense of calm and peacefulness. Two young men, an American and an Italian, appeared and explained that they would be telling us about life at Cenacolo and giving us their testimonies. I was immediately struck by Sean Corrigan, as he looked like a typical clean-cut preppy college student with his neat clothes and short blond hair. When he explained that he was a member of the community but originally came from Boston, the hairs stood up on the back of my neck. He spoke of how we are all 'called' to this place for a reason, and somehow I felt he was challenging me personally. It seemed an extraordinary coincidence that I should be on a pilgrimage for a little girl who was dying in Boston and should find him here, among a small community of recovering drug addicts from all over the world.

He told his story that day calmly, with humility and without any drama, and yet it left many of our pilgrim group in tears. I wrote in my diary that he was an example of what 'real faith has done, of what joy it brings', as he exuded joy and happiness. Seven years later, I decided to find him to see whether he still had that faith and the glow about him that I remembered so well and to tell him what his testimony had meant to me. I wanted to find out what it had felt like to reach rock bottom and what resources he had needed to survive.

I called the Cenacolo Community in Florida and was told that he was living nearby. He recalls the day I made contact and that it seemed to be somehow a message 'from God, that it would be God's work'. I met him off an aeroplane at La Guardia airport in New York, nervous that I wouldn't recognize him and that somehow it would be difficult to talk. How wrong I was. The same man walked towards me that I remembered from all those years ago, slightly greyer and a bit heavier but as gentle and humble as I remembered. He was happy to tell me his story but often found himself struggling with emotion.

'I grew up in a suburb of Boston, and I had three brothers – one older and two younger. My parents would be considered "middle class" in America; my dad was a computer analyst and my mum a nurse. We grew up in a Catholic family but it was mechanically Catholic. We went to Mass on Sunday; we did the basics, but there was nothing really from the heart that I could see anyway. Looking back, my parents definitely taught us good values, good morals and the basics, but you could see that things were done out of motion; they weren't done from their heart.

'When I was growing up, we had everything we needed. My parents definitely provided for us and they did really a great job. Looking back now, they were just awesome parents, you know. But even at a young age I had some wounds, and when I look back to try to understand why I started to take drugs in the first place, it wasn't because of how or where I grew up. I just remember that I had a feeling of emptiness inside me, and it's hard to explain but I think I was searching for something, for some kind of peace or meaning to my life, and drugs were the answer because they made me feel good, at least for a moment. I was so shy and timid and full of fear – I was unable to talk to girls, was unable to come out of myself, always wanted to be someone that I wasn't. It was all around us anyway where I grew up, a small place outside the city which has a good façade, but even today it has a bad name for drugs and alcohol and other family problems.

'I remember the first time I drank with a buddy of mine aged thirteen, and, you know, we'd get high and stuff and I remember feeling like this is the answer. I came out of myself; I was able go talk to people, be funny, overcome all those fears. It filled a void, and I know now it's all false, but at that time in my life at that young age it felt like it was an answer for me, if that makes sense. But things really progressed, and by the age of fifteen I was a full-blown alcoholic and cocaine addict. I was using cocaine on a daily basis, stealing and doing anything I really could to get my drug.

'My parents knew something was up, but they just didn't know how to help me. I would come home high; I would come home wasted. I remember when I was sixteen or seventeen they took me to a psychiatrist, tried different medications, but if anything they made things worse.

'Then at around twenty years old I had a kinda shake-up in my life – I had a drunk-driving arrest. I got into some trouble with the law and things shook me up, and this friend that I started using with, he started to get clean and sober and he helped me. For almost six years, I was able to stay clean and sober, even go to college and, in the end, find my wife. But during that time I was clean, I went after a lot of material things. I thought that getting a degree and getting a great job in construction management and having a beautiful wife and having an awesome pickup truck and the best stereo would give me happiness. I thought success and wealth instead of drugs would make me happy and fill the void inside me. But I just wasn't that happy; I just wasn't at rest; I just wasn't at peace.

'At twenty-six, right when I got married, that was really when my life fell apart. I started drinking again. I thought I could just have a couple of beers, but it just went on from there and my relapse was really quick. My drinking got out of hand, and I started taking painkillers and morphine for a shoulder injury and I abused them immediately. I never used the painkillers like I was supposed to; I used the excuse of my shoulder injury to get more drugs, and I just went out of control. I would justify myself by saying that it was a cocaine problem not an alcohol problem, or a problem with painkillers not with alcohol – all this just at the start of my marriage. My wife knew something was going on but she didn't know what to do. She was like, "Gosh, what's happening? We're newly married, you know – he's out of control."

'I was using so much morphine and so many painkillers and it was getting so expensive that I was taking my whole bank account, and I just couldn't pay the bills. For three or four years, things got worse. I couldn't pay for anything, and I just thought that instead of paying all this money for morphine, I could get heroin on the street. So I started sniffing heroin – it was cheaper – but I started to get so sick. I was so physically addicted that I couldn't function without it, literally – I couldn't get out of bed in the morning without having got high, and my wife was horrified. We were so far apart, she didn't know what to do, until one day I said, "I need to get help. I need to go to a detox. I need to do something; I'm totally addicted." I went to many different detoxes, many different clinics and rehabs. I did two weeks here, I did a week there, I did a month in another place, spending all different kinds of money, and they were giving me all different medicines to help, and I definitely learned a little but it just wasn't working.

'I was really sick. Even the doctors were saying, "You're probably not going to recover." I remember one doctor telling me, "Just stay on methadone the rest of your life, 'cause the chances of you getting clean from your heroin and painkiller and alcohol addiction are slim to none, and it's better for society in general that you just stay on methadone." Since then, I've dropped a letter to the doctor to tell him that I have recovered! So at that point things were just getting more and more hopeless and my wife didn't know what to do.

'Sometime during this period, my father actually went to Medjugorje and had an amazing conversion experience. My wife knew about it too, so in a kind of a last-ditch attempt to save me, she took me over there – I guess it was 1999 – and that was when I first visited the community [Cenacolo]. I remember I walked into the community chapel, and I heard two guys give a testimony and I said, "Yeh, this is awesome for them, but there's no way this is for me – there's no cigarettes around, no girls, no magazines, newspapers, TV. This is like the hard core way of getting clean." I said I could do it on my own – I didn't need that – and I guess it was my pride talking, but again, when I got back to Boston I relapsed. I was what they call a chronic relapser. Finally, my wife decided she had to kick me out of the house to make me get clean, so I was actually homeless.

'I lived on the street in a shelter, like a sober-house where people were supposed to stay clean, but I just couldn't do it. I kept falling and getting high again, and that community in Medjugorje, there's something that kept coming back to remind me. It was just a moment of grace when I knew that "OK, I need to do something 'cause I'm going to die," and I wanted to die, you know; I really was at the end. I just wanted to die: I had no hope; I had no reason for living. I remember just going to bed at night saying, "God, just take my life." I was totally desperate, so I called my wife and said, "I just need to get to Cenacolo. There's something telling me that I need to go to the community," and she put me in touch with the director in America, and he said to come for an interview at St Augustine in Florida. I showed up there; I was a mess and he let me in, and thank God he did. That was the first turning point in my life, when my life really started to change. I stayed there in the American community for two months.

'That time was very, very hard. I didn't sleep I don't think for the first thirty days, and I hardly knew what was going on around me. I had a guardian angel, the name given to the guy who stayed with me, the guy who came at night and stayed close to me and helped me out. I was detoxing with no other support, no medical intervention. I was really sick, but I'd been sick for the previous twelve months so it was nothing new, yet it was hard, though. I try never to forget how it was, 'cause if I remember that, it keeps me straight and reminds me that I never want to go through that again.

'After two months in America I was moved on to Medjugorje in Bosnia, and I remember thinking there was something going on there which brought me back to my childhood, like when I'd gone to Mass. The guys that had been in the community for a number of years all had smiles on their faces; they were all happy. I remember kneeling in the chapel for morning prayer and looking around and thinking, "What are we doing up at this hour? What's going on here? These people are crazy." I was like, "How could this be?" 'cause they didn't have a nice house or a nice car or wives with them.

'Most of my first days at Cenacolo, I was scared and aware of being miles from home. I was there for about ten days when I got in a fight with an Italian guy. I was so full of anger that anything they said, I just wanted to go at 'em. I actually packed my bag, got my passport and walked out into the middle of Medjugorje and decided I was going home. I thought this was a smart idea at the time so I went downtown and begged for money and got enough to call home to tell my wife I'm coming home. I remember she said, "What are you doing? You need to go back and finish the programme, and you're not welcome home." I knew that was hard for her to say, but I actually went away to get my ticket changed, and I was just thinking of heading home and starting over perhaps in some other part of America.

'I remember I spent about ten days living on the streets of Medjugorje, just surviving, until one day I went into St James's Church in the middle of town and I just said, "God, what am I supposed to do...?" I just knew I had to go back to the community. I had realized I wasn't ready to leave when I started to wonder whether I could get heroin in Mostar or Sarajevo, and I realized I was gonna use again which really scared me. I may have been physically clean, but mentally and spiritually I wasn't ready.

'They welcomed me back to the community and I started again. It was hard, you know; the guys really, really broke me and gave me a hard time about doing it my way. My excuse was I wanted to see my wife, but that kind of fell apart 'cause she didn't want to see me how I was. I remember being in the chapel and feeling like I was totally broken and I literally had nothing. I mean, I couldn't escape. I don't know how to describe it – it was like I felt completely naked. I was always used to having some way to escape, whether it was alcohol, drugs, girls, cigarettes, telephone, TV – some distraction to escape. And at this point, I just had this clear thought: it was just me and God there, and I needed to do something. I needed to do what the guys around me started to tell me and to really start trusting and realizing that God had a plan for me and that my life was worthwhile.

'I couldn't run anymore. I couldn't hide anymore; there was no more hiding. I had to face the facts that I was a severe addict and a severe drug addict, not just a guy who went out and did recreational drugs a few times. I was heavily addicted to hard-core drugs and I had two choices: to go back to my old lifestyle, which would essentially mean dying – even my doctor said it was a miracle that I was alive with the amount of drugs that I was taking – or that I start to do the things that the community was suggesting and really begin to have a new life and to have a relationship with God.

'It was just a moment of clarity I guess I can call it, where I said that even though I don't have any joy – I'm not happy, I don't have much hope – there was still something inside me that knew that I had to make that decision to choose life. That was a real turning point for me when I accepted this. I put both feet inside the community and not one outside and one inside. I put both feet inside and said, "God, I really don't know you, but I want to understand what's going on here," and at that point when I started to open myself, people around me started opening up to me and things started to get real; I really started to understand. It wasn't a bolt of lightning that came down, but it was the beginning of many revelations on life itself and my relationship with God.

'One thing I clearly remember after eight months there was that I hadn't heard anything from my family. I remember really starting to pray for my wife and feeling so guilty about all the mistakes and how I had destroyed my family. I really did pray hard, and then I got my first letter from the outside. It was from my wife, and I found out that she was in Italy. I read it and found out that everything's fine, that she still loved me, and not only did she love me but she had actually entered another community in order to help her understand what I was going through. She had met Sister Elvira in America and asked how she could help me, and Elvira had suggested joining a women's house in Italy even though she didn't have any of the problems they did. I was totally crying and crying in the chapel, and I just thought, "Thank God."

'I came to find out that my wife was living the same life I was over in Italy, and I was absolutely blown away. She had sacrificed her own life and comfort to make things work for us. She had always had a great faith in God and believed in our marriage and the vows we took. Sister Elvira has since used Elaine's name many times when talking about love and sacrifice. Soon after that it was Sister Elvira's birthday, and a lot of the houses from around Europe go to this one central point in Italy for a big festival and they celebrate her birthday, and I was allowed to go. I was so excited 'cause I knew I was going to see my wife there and she was singing in the choir. It was just awesome, and we spent the whole weekend together talking, and I remember saying how sorry I was, and there was such forgiveness and love and there was a joy there that was beyond belief... I'll never forget it... I just knew everything would be OK, and it was a joy that I looked for in alcohol and that I looked for in drugs and that I looked for in material things that I just never found. But in that moment when I saw my wife and we hugged, it was like

173

a joy from God. It's something that I still can't describe to this day. I just knew it was going to be OK.

'It was amazing. I realized I hadn't known how to let someone love me, let alone love someone else. I mean it was overwhelming, yet I realized that not only did God love me, but my wife loved me, and I needed to start to like myself and to start to love other people around me. I mean, that was the most concrete example of love that I'd ever seen in my life. It was right there in front of me and it happened at that moment; it just clicked, like she gave up her whole career, her whole life for the sake of our marriage, for the sake of me. My wife had a good faith and had always prayed her whole life, but now she was transformed also through the community.

'After that weekend, I had to leave her to return to Medjugorje, and that was just the longest bus ride but I knew I needed to continue and finish what I had started, something I had not done much of in my life. I was hoping to get transferred to Italy after a few months, but I ended up getting a bad lung infection that summer and having to be sent to America for eighteen months for treatment.

'I remember giving testimonies that spring before I got ill but after seeing my wife – including the one that you [Julia] would have heard. I was nervous every time, but I always felt good after I talked, 'cause I felt I was sharing something, that I was sharing hope, and I also felt that God would tell me what to say, if that makes sense. I would speak from the heart, and there were many times when I was talking and there was a moment of illumination where I knew that I was saying something that somebody needed to hear. Giving a testimony in front of a group of people is a very powerful thing. That's why Elvira always said, "Say a prayer before and make sure that you're focused and you're talking from your heart and you're living in truth and make sure you're clean." You were always asked at short notice and you'd have to run to your house, wash your hands, wash your face and put on a collar and shirt and go talk, very unprepared. It really started to help me; talking helped make things concrete and real.

'I've seen so many people's lives change in Medjugorje and so many things happen, not just with my own life. I believe I'm a miracle, and yet I also know that one thing I really, really understand is my weaknesses. I understand that I'm just one bad decision away from falling. I just believe you can make a choice for good or for evil, and I think that spiritual forces are definitely real – the devil on your right shoulder and the angel on your left. One thing the community really taught me is to know my limits and to know my weaknesses and to know the places I can't go, the people I can't hang out with. I need to surround myself with prayer and to live a kind of radical lifestyle. I'm an ex-heroin addict; I can't just have a mediocre life and keep my head above water. Plenty of people think I am crazy to be praying three rosaries a day – that is crazy to 99 per cent of Catholics – but I need to do it and it gives me joy and happiness and that void in me doesn't exist anymore. I'm really at peace. There are days that I flip over like anyone, but I feel like I'm really at peace.

'After I became ill and returned to America for treatment, I was able to keep in touch with my wife. We were writing a letter every month, and she soon returned to Boston to be closer to me, although we only met a couple of times a year. Our marriage was becoming stronger and stronger even though we were far apart. Sister Elvira's idea was that I had to do my full three-year walk alone in the community and that my wife can be by my side but not physically, and at the end of that time we would renew our wedding vows. We both went back to Italy to different houses and assumed we would just be there a couple of weeks, but we were made to wait almost eight months. During that time, we would work together during the day but be separated at night, which was a real struggle. Suddenly we were called to see Elvira, and she told us we could renew our vows the very next day, the day of Pentecost 2003, in front of thousands of people. We were both so happy.

'After your time in Cenacolo, Sister Elvira gives you an opportunity to "give back". You can do that by helping other addicts around you or going to one of the mission houses in South America. We did both by helping addicts first in Florida and then by staying in the mission in Brazil. We were like parents to about ten orphaned children aged from four to twelve who lived in the house. We took care of all their needs and we loved them all, especially an eight-year-old called Lucas, who had been abandoned at six months old and severely abused. He really captured our hearts and loved being with us twenty-four hours a day. We learned so much from the children; they are real professors of life. At last we could be a married couple, and it was an awesome experience. We had our struggles as we rediscovered each other, but we discovered that our love and our faith were really strong, that we had found something really awesome here. It was a great gift to work with the children, although there were many trials, dealing with a different culture and language, and we were so busy from five in the morning until you crashed into bed. It was a time for us to give back as we felt we had been given so many gifts, but in reality they gave us so much more.

'In the end, we had to return to America as Elaine was really sick. She actually has painful endometriosis, and in Brazil she got really, really sick, and we went to the doctor. They did an ultrasound and told us she had these huge cysts and needed a major operation back in Florida, so we moved back to the Cenacolo house there. She got an operation, but doctors were saying, "You know, she'll not be able to get pregnant, but at least this will help her pain." We wanted to stay in Brazil, but with her health, it was very stressful in the mission. We started to pray and really felt that we were called to life outside, to restart our life… It wasn't something we just decided overnight.

'We left the community with nothing but two duffel bags, yet we had everything. We were so happy, but we had no material things – we had no money, I mean, not a nickel. They gave us a little gas money and let us borrow a car for a month and the house for a month, and I rolled up my sleeves and started working for a man whose daughter is in the community, and Elaine got a job as a teacher, and we were saving up money so we could get our own apartment. Overall, I had spent six years – not just the usual three – as part of the community. For six years, I was with people every day, and I woke up at six and at six fifteen I'm in the chapel. I mean it was just a set, hard schedule and here I am now driving to work alone but knowing that I have to put God first in my life. I need to do the same things that I learned in community: to live honestly, to try to be humble, to admit my mistakes, to share profoundly with my wife the things that are going on and to be honest with that and, most importantly, to pray. That's what we still do every day, and I know that's my life saviour, you know, it's like my medicine. I have a terminal illness, and if I don't take my medicine, I will die. I've relapsed twenty times in my life, and I don't need that to happen again; I need to protect myself in prayer.

'Even now, I can be on a construction site and the guys are drinking beers, and a moment comes across me and I think that looks good, so, again, I think I have that padding around me, the prayer that protects me. I'm able to look at it and think, "Wait a minute – if I drink that beer it will lead to six beers, which will lead to a line of cocaine, which will lead to a pill, heroin, I'm homeless, I'm in the gutter... or I'm dead." So I'm able to think things through, to realize I don't *need* it. I've found happiness and joy in my relationship with God. I've found that in real love. I've found that in my relationships with other people. I really feel that there's been a fulfilment, you know, and such happiness and joy in my life and it just keeps getting better. We went back to Medjugorje in 2006 for Christmas and

New Year to give thanks, and when we were there we decided to give up our wish to have a baby and to accept that as our cross, but suddenly we discover Elaine's pregnant... in January, right after we got back from Medjugorje, and it was like joy after joy and it's a miracle. We'd been married eleven years then, and she was told she definitely couldn't get pregnant; it was just awesome. Our little girl is called Mary Elizabeth as a reminder of the moving visitation of Mary, mother of Jesus, to her cousin Elizabeth, who also had the special blessing of bearing a child.

'Now we go to the Florida community house every week and it's good for me, because I see the new guys enter and I'm able to give them hope but they can help me a lot more, 'cause when I see a new guy come in who's sick or he can't sleep at night or he's miserable, I know that that could be me but for the grace of God. If there is one really important thing for people to know it is that you're never too far gone for God. No matter how low you are, no matter how ruined and soiled and dirty and in the gutter you are, you're still so loved by God. When I was in the gutter with the needle in my arm, God was with me; he was just waiting for me to turn around and to turn back to him.

'If I think about my epitaph, I would want St Augustine's line that I love: "Our heart is restless until it rests in you, O Lord." I don't believe that we can find true peace until we encounter the Lord; he is the only one who can fill our emptiness and give us meaning. I have two favourite psalms from the Bible: Psalm 46, beginning, "God is our refuge and strength, a very present help in trouble," and Psalm 118, "The Lord is my strength and my might; he has become my salvation." I realize that I am clean and sober today and that I am at peace because of his strength, not my own.'

This story may seem almost unreal and very hard to read. All I know is that Sean's testimony had a remarkable impact on me; it was a 'life-changing moment', as I wrote in my diary. At that time in my life, I was relying only on my own diminishing inner strength and, like many, keeping up a façade that I had created of confidence and efficiency. I saw it as a weakness to show how I really felt, to admit my own insecurities and growing sense of panic. Many of us can sympathize with Sean's feeling of emptiness, even feeling unlovable at times. His words strike a chord, inspiring people to change their lives. I had felt such a need to unburden myself as I arrived in Medjugorje, but I saw how important it was to listen and learn from other people's stories. One of the great lessons to take away from Cenacolo is that true healing can happen when we rid our lives of unnecessary burdens and perhaps even accept that sometimes we have to suffer in order to grow as people and to appreciate the gift of life that we have.

Listening to Sean in 2001, I realized how easy it is to judge other people for their addictions or their homelessness without any understanding or compassion. It would have been possible for my life to have taken a similar turn, as had happened to other people I knew. In my own way, I had been addicted to my egocentric working life, to the buzz it gave me, and had always considered the idea of slowing down to be a sign of weakness. If it had not been for my own turning point that started with Cameron, maybe I, too, would have needed the kind of jolt that someone like Olivia Giles got in her life, a dramatic and terrible illness that forced her to slow down.

Hearing Sean's story was very moving, particularly the contrast between his public admission of his own weakness and the faith and conviction that shone out of his face. The image of Sean lying in the gutter, with God just waiting for him to turn around to him, made a deep impression on me.

I was also struck by the transformational love of his wife Elaine, who sacrificed so much for her marriage. It is easy to underestimate the power of love in our lives, the love that we receive but also that we give to others. Sean tells an extraordinary story of hope when all hope seemed lost, of a man who came so close to death and yet chose to live again. Both Sean and Elaine have suffered tremendously, and yet they emerged from their suffering to make such a positive contribution to our world. As I see photographs of the joyful Corrigan family in Florida today, I just hope that their daughter will one day know how lucky she is to have such remarkable parents.

CONCLUSION

Accepted wisdom in our society seems to be that people are what they are, good or bad, and never really fundamentally change. And yet I've learned on this journey that many people experience turning points: an impetus of some kind that completely and utterly changes the course and focus of their lives. Some come out of extremely challenging moments, while others from a gradual understanding that life is not as it should be. If we recognize these turning points, they can be an opportunity for us to change our lives, a second chance, a way to rediscover a new awareness of ourselves and what we can mean to others. In a world that is starting to question the value of success, wealth and fame, this is even more important.

As I explored the lives and stories of those I have included in this book, common themes and lessons emerged. It seems clear to me that some suffering can have a purpose, that choosing a life where you make a difference to others can bring great joy, and that a strong character, courage and often faith are key to a meaningful response. Many who have survived traumatic experiences feel gratitude for all that they have and have an ability to make the best of their situation.

Several people in this book have suffered terrible loss or injury. Gordon Brown, Bob Geldof, Diane Irabaruta and the Lord family have all had to adapt to a life without loved ones, and I still find it hard to imagine the reality of the pain that the loss of a child brings. Chris Moon and Olivia Giles had disabilities forced on them that would destroy many people, and yet they retain an incredibly positive outlook and a determination not to be victims of their circumstances. Sean and Franny became drug addicts and were lucky to recover and make something of their lives. Clive and

John responded to obvious injustice and unfairness in the world, while Paula has been lucky to escape the negative impact of her role as a carer at a very young age.

All their stories share a common theme, a common humanity and a hopefulness. However bad life has been for them, it is obvious that their suffering has had some kind of purpose, a positive outcome of some kind. For young women like Diane Irabaruta and Paula Lowther, that purpose may only just be becoming clear, but for the others there is no doubt that they are changing the world for the better. Gordon Brown, Bob Geldof and John Wood are making a difference to the lives of children across the world and inspiring others to get involved. Olivia Giles and Chris Moon have contributed a significant amount to charity in a variety of ways. Clive Stafford Smith saves lives and fights for freedom. Franny McGrath and Sean Corrigan live out their faith every day serving others.

In every case, it is clear that the work these remarkable individuals do makes a difference to their own lives and the way they feel about themselves. It is visibly obvious in the faces of men like Sean and Clive. It has been essential to the recoveries of both Franny and Sean and will be the key to Paula's future. For those who have had a particularly tough childhood, helping others is important for their own confidence and self-esteem, as we have learned many times over at ProjectScotland.

Reading these stories, it is impossible not to feel great admiration for the courage that so many have shown in the face of adversity, but equally, it takes courage for ordinary people to step out of a comfortable and safe existence to change their lives. Some people are lucky to be born to parents who are good role models or with the kind of strong character that Olivia or Diane has. It can work against them at times but is invaluable in a crisis. Others have to face and accept their own weaknesses and addictions, to learn from them and find the strength to fight back, perhaps, like Sean and Franny, with the armour of their faith. Others simply need to be aware of who they are and be prepared to take a small step towards a new goal and purpose in life.

From my own perspective, I find it hard to imagine life now without my faith. I no longer take it for granted and know it takes effort to keep it strong. Just as I try to look after my physical and emotional welfare, I have to work at my spiritual health by attending church, reading my Bible and taking time out for prayer and pilgrimages, but it is always a challenge. It has not been important to every individual in this book and many resent aspects of formal religion, but I sense that a general spiritual awareness is relevant, even in the fervently atheistic world of Bob Geldof. In my view these individuals walk in the path of Christ, a man of humility but great strength, a man who suffered so much but was always loving and compassionate, fighting injustice and intolerance. He taught us the only kind of success that matters is to live a meaningful life in the service of others, to love and to be loved.

After the death of my much admired father-in-law, Angus Ogilvy, we found in his Bible a definition of success, which is commonly attributed to Ralph Waldo Emerson. Many of the individuals in this book are lucky enough to have found this kind of fulfilment.

Success

To laugh often and much;

To win the respect of intelligent people and the affection of children;

*To earn the appreciation of honest critics and
endure the betrayal of false friends;*

*To appreciate beauty,
To find the best in others;*

*To leave the world a bit better, whether by a healthy child,
a garden patch or a redeemed social condition;*

To know even one life has breathed easier because you have lived.

This is to have succeeded.

APPENDIX:

CHARITIES AND COURSES MENTIONED IN THIS BOOK

PROJECTSCOTLAND

Profits from the sale of this book will go to ProjectScotland, a national charity that provides opportunities for young people to realize their potential through full-time volunteering for up to six months.

Through ProjectScotland, 16 to 25-year-olds can choose from a variety of meaningful and rewarding projects within a wide range of not-for-profit organizations that fit their interests. Every young person has a mentor to support and help them in their transition into employment or further education and receives living expenses.

Volunteers gain confidence and important life skills through helping others in their community as well as raised aspirations and better employment prospects. Many come from the most deprived areas of Scotland. They describe the satisfaction of 'feeling valued, realizing you are good at something when your school record says otherwise, feeling confident and getting a buzz out of helping others in the community around you'.

Since it was founded in 2005, almost 3,000 young people have achieved 2 million hours of volunteering all over Scotland and contributed over £21 million to the Scottish economy in 07/08, boosting the activities of many charities. The trustees and staff can be very proud of this achievement, but funding will be the challenge for the years ahead. ProjectScotland is a secular organization that looks for support from central government and local authorities as well as trusts, foundations, companies and individuals.

If you wish to know more about the organization, or to consider giving it your support, please see our website at www.projectscotland.co.uk, email info@projectscotland.co.uk or call 0131 226 0700. For information about any of the other organizations mentioned, please refer to their websites.

Cameron and Hayden Lord Foundation

The mission of the Foundation is to decrease the incidence of chronic and complex childhood diseases and to increase the quality of emotional, spiritual and medical care for families facing these diseases, including a project to educate nursing leaders in paediatric palliative care. Cameron and Hayden died of Tay-Sachs disease, and more information on this and other related diseases can be found at www.ntsad.org. Website: www.lordfoundation.org.

Columba 1400

Founded in Staffin on the Isle of Skye in 2000, Columba 1400 is a social enterprise devoted to leadership development. The core purpose is to release the potential of young people from 'tough realities' who have suffered significant personal and social challenges, particularly those leaving care. Over 3,500 people have taken part in a range of programmes, including those who are making a difference to the lives of young people, such as head teachers.
Website: www.columba1400.com.

The Cenacolo Community

Founded in 1983 by Sister Elvira Petrozzi to help drug addicts and lost youth. The main headquarters are in Italy, but there are now twenty-seven fraternities all over the world, accommodating over 600 men and women, all rediscovering the gifts of work, friendship and faith as a solution to their problems.
Website: www.comunitacenacolo.it
For the UK: www.cenacolofriends.org.uk

500 Miles

Founded in 2007 by Olivia Giles and Jamie Andrew (both Scottish quadruple amputees) to support amputees and other disabled

people in deprived areas of the world. The particular focus is on the development and delivery of prosthetic and orthotic services and other mobility/function-promoting services, such as orthopaedic and plastic surgery, all designed to get people moving. The initial projects are in Malawi and Zambia.
Website: www.500miles.co.uk.

The Jennifer Brown Research Fund

The Fund supports groundbreaking research to save newborn lives and solve pregnancy problems. A talented team of scientists based in Edinburgh are advancing research projects that are making real progress towards resolving some of the life-threatening complications that can arise during pregnancy. The Fund is supported by PiggyBankKids, a children's charity set up in 2002 that creates opportunities for children and young people who would otherwise miss out.
Website: www.piggybankkids.org.

Miracles

A British charity that provides hope to all those for whom the hope of a miracle is their only alternative to despair. It provides crisis funding in situations of dire and multiple distress and terminal illness, a priority for those in the UK who fall through the net of other aid agencies. Miracles runs a mission in Bosnia to provide help to the poorest of the poor, providing medical treatment, housing, education and a new Centre for Prosthesis and Care in one of the worst land-mined countries in the world.
Website: www.miraclesthecharity.org.

Perth and District YMCA

The YMCA organization in Scotland works with over 12,000 young people every week, including those who are struggling to cope with issues such as drugs, alcohol, family crises, housing, offending and other forms of antisocial behaviour. They are

there to serve the needs of the most vulnerable and excluded from our communities.
Website: www.ymcascotland.org.

Reprieve

Reprieve was founded in 1999 to help prisoners awaiting execution, those wrongly imprisoned as a result of the 'war on terror' (particularly in Guantanamo Bay) and to raise the profile of all abuses of human rights. Reprieve's lawyers investigate, litigate and educate. They work on the front line, providing legal support to prisoners unable to pay for it themselves.
Website: www.reprieve.org.uk.

Room to Read

Room to Read was established in 2000, based on the belief that education is crucial to breaking the cycle of poverty in the developing world. Since then, the organization has supported nearly 2 million children by providing better access to education. Room to Read has catalysed the construction of more than 700 schools and 7,000 bilingual libraries with 5 million books, and continues to support over 7,000 girls through secondary school. Room to Read is providing opportunities that change children's lives and communities throughout Bangladesh, Cambodia, India, Laos, Nepal, South Africa, Sri Lanka, Vietnam and Zambia.
Website: www.roomtoread.org.

Comfort Rwanda

A Scottish organization established in 1999 – five years after the genocide – to help Rwandan Christian partners in their work to support survivors. Activities include providing cattle and goats, funding education, sponsoring orphan families, famine relief, funding trauma healing camps, building wells and houses, and community development projects.
Website: www.comfortrwanda.org.uk.

Alpha

Over 2 million people in the UK and 11 million worldwide have now attended an Alpha Course, an opportunity to explore the meaning of life in a relaxed setting over a ten-week period. It runs in thousands of churches of all denominations as well as in prisons, universities, gyms and offices.
Website: www.uk.alpha.org.

The Hoffman Process

An eight-day intensive and confidential residential course of personal discovery and development. It helps individuals to examine and better understand their lives and reveals why they behave the way they do. More than 70,000 people around the world have used the Hoffman techniques to improve their quality of life and restore their relationships with friends and family.
Website: www.hoffmaninstitute.co.uk.

About the Author

Julia Ogilvy is founder and chairman of ProjectScotland, a revolutionary national volunteering organization for 16 to 25-year-olds. She won a number of awards in her previous role as Managing Director of Hamilton and Inches, including Scottish Businesswoman of the Year, and was a finalist in the Veuve Clicquot Businesswoman of the Year Award. More recently she won the Ernst & Young Scottish Social Entrepeneur of the Year Award for her work with ProjectScotland. She is a member of the Prime Minister's Council for Social Action, an elder in the Church of Scotland, on the board of Lloyds TSB Scotland and works with various charities. She lives in Scotland with her husband, two children and three chickens.

For more information about this book, and to share stories, visit www.turning-pointsonline.com